I0460172

# TruResilience:
## The Ultimate Step-by-Step Guide to Reprogramming Your Mindset and Transforming Your Life

A Rapid Route for Those Rebuilding After Trauma, Incarceration, or Devastating Loss—Using Neuroscience, Psychology, and Practical Action

Jackie Truman

# Table of Contents

# Introduction

# The Moment Everything Changes

*"Your life does not get better by chance, it gets better by change."* – Jim Rohn

There was a time when I believed that suffering was just the way things were—a relentless cycle of disappointment, failure, and rejection that I somehow deserved. I thought if I could just escape, start over in a new place, erase my past, then maybe, just maybe, I could outrun the weight of everything that had gone wrong. But no matter how many times I tried to reposition myself to go in the opposite direction, I only seemed to collide head-on with another catastrophe. My life felt like one train wreck after another.

As someone who has personally navigated the challenges of living with a past that society often views as a permanent stain, I understand the struggle of feeling like your history defines you. This sense of hopelessness is familiar to many who have faced systemic barriers or personal crises. However, it's crucial to recognize that these challenges are not insurmountable. By understanding how our minds work and taking control of our narratives, we can begin to rewrite our stories and reclaim our power. This book is designed to guide you through that process, providing tools to transform your life from one of struggle to one of resilience and success.

## Why This Book Matters

This book isn't here to offer empty platitudes or surface-level self-help fluff. It's not another "think positive" manifesto that leaves you momentarily inspired but fundamentally unchanged. This is for those who have been to hell and back, those who know what it's like to have doors slammed in their face, to be told they'll never recover, to fight against a world that would rather see them stay broken. It contains real life case studies in each chapter that demonstrates the resilience of these individuals and how they incorporated these themes to reprogram their mind and rebuild their lives. This book is a blueprint—not just for healing, but for reclaiming your power, rewriting your story, and designing a life that no longer feels like a series of punishments.

## The Science Behind Transformation

Society is quick to brand certain people as lost causes. Those with criminal records, those from broken homes, those who have suffered trauma, poverty, addiction, incarceration—people whose pasts are worn like a permanent stain that the world refuses to let them wash clean. The truth, though, is that change isn't just possible; it's inevitable when you understand how the mind works. Neuroscience has proven that the brain is malleable. Studies on neuroplasticity show that no matter how deep the mental grooves of failure and self-sabotage may seem, they can be rewritten. Your past does not have to dictate your future—unless you let it.

## What You Will Learn

Through a combination of neuroscience, psychology, and real-world strategies, this book will guide you through a transformative journey. Here's what you can expect to learn:

1. **Breaking the Cycle of Self-Doubt:** In Chapter 1, you'll discover how to identify and break the subconscious beliefs keeping you stuck. You'll learn to shift from a victim mindset to a leader's mindset, no matter where you're starting from.

2. **Rewiring Your Brain for Success:** Chapter 2 explores the neuroscience of transformation, teaching you how to break the habit of being your old self and adopt a success mindset.

3. **Overcoming Fear and Self-Doubt:** Chapter 3 helps you understand the root of fear and shows you how to overcome the fear of failure, rejection, and even success itself.

4. **Breaking Free from Toxic Patterns:** Chapter 4 guides you in

identifying toxic people and environments and creating a positive, growth-oriented space around you.

5. **Mastering Self-Discipline and Productivity:** Chapter 5 teaches you how to develop unstoppable self-discipline and productivity without relying on motivation.

6. **Financial Success and Wealth Mindset Transformation:** Chapter 6 shows you how to master your finances and build real wealth, even if you've been financially devastated.

7. **Developing Unshakable Confidence:** Chapter 7 helps you develop unshakable confidence and command respect in any room.

8. **Making Success Automatic:** Finally, Chapter 8 provides strategies for making your success permanent by locking in identity-based habits and creating systems that ensure lasting transformation.

## Your Turning Point Starts Here

If you've ever felt like the world wrote your story for you, this is your chance to take the pen back. It won't be easy. There will be days when old habits creep in, when fear whispers that you're wasting your time, when people who have never walked your path try to convince you that change isn't possible for someone like you. Ignore them. People will always judge you based on the version of you they remember. That is their limitation, not yours. The only thing that matters is who you decide to be now.

The moment you commit to rewriting your story, everything begins to shift. This is your invitation to rise. To take the lessons from your past, the pain, the failures, the moments you thought would break you—and turn them into fuel. Every chapter includes tools you can employ to see real change take shape in your life. You don't have to try everything, but rather find what resonates with you and add it to your toolbox.

Welcome to your new beginning.

Welcome to **TruResilience.**

# Chapter 1

# Breaking the Cycle – Why You Keep Failing (And How to Stop)

*"Insanity is doing the same thing over and over and expecting different results."* – Albert Einstein

For many of us, failure isn't about not trying hard enough; it's about unseen forces that dictate our actions before we even realize it. The real culprit behind repeated setbacks isn't a lack of effort—it's the hidden mindset programming that shapes our decisions. This chapter is about exposing those scripts and rewriting them. It's about breaking free from unconscious mental patterns shaped by trauma, loss, or oppression and reclaiming control over the choices we make each day.

Until we recognize the cycles keeping us trapped, we remain prisoners of circumstances that were never meant to define us. The journey to breaking these cycles begins with understanding how our minds operate and how we can take back control. In this chapter, you'll discover exactly how to recognize and rewrite the subconscious beliefs and emotional traps that keep you stuck, so you can finally break free and reclaim control of your life.

## Preview – Meet Jay Jordan

Imagine feeling trapped—not just physically, but emotionally and mentally— caught in the loop of negative habits, repeated mistakes, and limiting beliefs. Jay Jordan knows this cycle intimately. At 18, he found himself facing years behind bars. But Jay made one powerful decision: to change the internal narrative that kept him trapped. His journey from inmate to advocate shows us that it's never too late to rewrite your story.

You'll discover Jay's full story at the end of this chapter, and learn exactly how he applied these principles to transform his life.

## 1.1 The Hidden Mindset Programming That Holds You Back

Our minds function like sophisticated machines, with most of their programming running beneath the surface. Imagine driving a car where nearly every function—steering, acceleration, braking—is automated, leaving you with only the illusion of control. That's how our subconscious functions, dictating up to 95% of our actions without our awareness. This programming isn't just a product of personal experience; it's shaped by upbringing, social conditions, systemic barriers, and trauma. It determines how we react to opportunities, how we interpret failure, and whether we believe we deserve success at all.

For example, those impacted by the criminal justice system might have a script that says, "You will always be defined by your worst mistake." For those raised in poverty, it might be, "Security is not for people like you." These silent beliefs shape decisions before we even realize we are making them. The first step to breaking the cycle is exposing these hidden narratives.

### Your Subconscious Is Running the Show

To illustrate this, visualize how our daily routines are influenced by subconscious patterns. Every morning, we wake up and move through familiar motions— the same coffee cup, the same route to work, the same reactions to stress. These ingrained patterns control everything from minor habits to critical life decisions.

Dr. John Bargh's groundbreaking research, detailed in his 2017 book, *Before You Know It: The Unconscious Reasons We Do What We Do*, illuminates how our behavior is profoundly influenced by unconscious cues. Our environment, past traumas, and deeply ingrained beliefs operate in the background, shaping our choices without our awareness. Bargh's work reveals that these hidden mental processes govern our actions in various domains, from race relations to business decisions.

For someone who has experienced repeated rejection—whether from the job market, the housing system, or personal relationships—this unconscious programming might manifest as self-sabotage. Thoughts like "Why apply if I won't get hired?" or "Why try if I'm going to fail?" are not objective truths; rather, they are learned responses that can be unlearned. Bargh's research suggests that these automatic thoughts are akin to psychological "auto-pilot" responses, formed through repeated experiences that strengthen neural associations between rejection cues and defeatist thoughts.

Think of your subconscious as a well-worn path in the woods. It takes no effort to walk it because it has been traveled so many times before. This is why, despite our best intentions, we keep falling into the same cycles. Breaking the cycle requires forging an entirely new path, one that at first feels unnatural and exhausting. The good news? With enough repetition, this new path becomes the default.

## The Silent Influencer: When Your Mind Works Against You

Our subconscious does not distinguish between what helps us and what harms us—it simply reinforces what it has been taught. If you've been conditioned to believe that stability is unattainable, every attempt to create it will feel unnatural. If you've been raised in an environment where financial insecurity was the norm, wealth may subconsciously feel unsafe. This is why self-sabotage isn't about a lack of willpower—it's about deeply ingrained protective mechanisms that were once necessary but are no longer serving you.

Dr. Joe Dispenza explains it this way: *"When you become aware of the unconscious patterns that control your behavior, you have the power to change them."* Awareness is the first weapon against subconscious sabotage. Once you see the pattern, you can break it.

The crazy part is, we all know it's there. Well-versed scripts we share with others, often disguised as sarcastic quips. When you choose to identify this programming, you'll see patterns emerge—fear of success, hesitance to trust others, defaulting to survival mode even when safety was available. This awareness can be painful, but it is also the beginning of true change. When I became serious about getting out of survival mode, I found the code behind my self-destruction, and with that knowledge, I could begin rewriting it.

## Why Positive Thinking Isn't Enough

We've all heard it before: *"Just think positive!"* A phrase tossed around as if optimism alone has the power to undo years of struggle, systemic barriers, and deep-rooted trauma. While the intention behind the mantra is often well-meaning, the reality is far more complex. When you've hit rock bottom—whether due to systemic injustice, financial devastation, the lasting weight of a criminal record, or the immeasurable pain of loss—being told to simply "stay positive" can feel like an insult.

## Beyond Surface-Level Optimism

Imagine standing in front of a house that has been battered by storms for years—roof caving in, foundation cracked, walls buckling under the weight of past damage. Now imagine someone handing you a bucket of paint and telling you to "spruce it up." That's what surface-level positivity does. It offers a fresh coat of encouragement, but it doesn't repair the damage beneath. No matter how bright the color, the structural weaknesses remain.

This is why so many people feel defeated after trying to adopt a positive mindset, only to find themselves slipping back into despair. Research in cognitive psychology confirms that forced positivity without addressing deeper, underlying beliefs is ineffective. Dr. Barbara Fredrickson, a leading researcher in positive psychology, states, *"Positive emotions broaden your awareness, but they need to be anchored in deeper, meaningful change to create lasting transformation."* Without this anchoring, optimism remains a temporary high—fleeting and fragile in the face of real obstacles.

For those who have lived through hardship, systemic failure, or deep personal crisis, the problem isn't a lack of positive thinking. It's that the weight of past experiences has built a subconscious program that overrides conscious intention. You may want to believe in your ability to succeed, but if every past experience has reinforced the opposite, optimism alone is a battle fought with empty weapons.

## The Battle Within

If success were only a matter of choosing to think positively, far more people would have broken free from poverty, discrimination, and the lasting effects of systemic oppression. But beneath every outward attempt at self-improvement lies an internal war—a fight between the person you want to become and the deeply ingrained conditioning that insists you stay where you are.

Your logical, goal-oriented self wants to believe you can rebuild. It sets ambitious plans, envisions a better future, and longs for change. But your subconscious? It's wired to survive based on what it has known. If it has only known struggle, failure, and rejection, it clings to those experiences as a blueprint for how the world operates.

I know this battle intimately. There was a time when I desperately tried to move forward—new goals, new habits, new declarations of *"this time will be different."* But no matter how much effort I put in, something pulled me back. I'd self-sabotage opportunities, shrink in the face of progress, and retreat into old patterns as if some unseen force demanded it. Every attempt at progress feels like walking against an invisible current. It's exhausting. And if you don't understand why it's happening, you start to believe that you are the problem. You aren't. The problem is the subconscious script running in the background—one that was likely written long before you had a choice in the matter. I later learned that force had a name: *conditioning.*

## The Illusion of Change

Motivational speeches, self-help affirmations, and vision boards all have their place. But without deep internal work, they remain little more than temporary morale boosters. You might feel a surge of hope after reading an inspiring quote or attending a seminar, but what happens the next morning? The same doubts creep in. The same barriers still exist. The same subconscious patterns dictate your choices.

It's not that these tools are useless—it's that they only scratch the surface. Real change isn't about masking wounds; it's about healing them. Neuroscience has shown that real transformation happens at the level of *neural pathways*—the connections in our brains that determine how we think, feel, and react. Dr. Joe Dispenza, a pioneer in neuroplasticity, explains:

*"You cannot think greater than how you feel. If your emotions are rooted in the past, your thoughts will follow. Change comes when you train your body to feel a new reality before it arrives."*

This means rewiring isn't just about *thinking* differently. It's about feeling different—deep in your core, at a level where your past no longer dictates your future.

## Breaking Free from the Cycle

I remember when I first began using affirmations, believing they would be the key to transforming my mindset. I wrote them down, repeated them daily, and held onto them like a lifeline. But within days of stopping, my old fears returned. The affirmations hadn't failed me—I had simply never gone deep enough to confront the subconscious programming that was fighting against them.

It was only when I started questioning the *why* behind my self-doubt—digging into the roots of my belief system and challenging the old narratives I had absorbed—that the real shift began. It wasn't an overnight process. It required peeling back layers of fear, shame, and ingrained limitations. But for the first time, the changes were *real*.

If you've ever felt like you're stuck in the same cycle despite your best efforts, know this: It's not a lack of willpower. It's not a personal failure. It's conditioning. And the good news? Conditioning can be rewritten.

## How Your Identity Shapes Your Success

Your identity is the blueprint of your reality. It's not just the lens through which you see the world—it's the filter through which the world responds to you. The way you define yourself, the story you tell about who you are, and the beliefs you hold about your worthiness create the boundaries of your potential. If you've been labeled a failure, an outsider, or "damaged goods" by society, those messages seep into your subconscious, shaping the decisions you make and the risks you avoid. Identity becomes more than just self-perception. It becomes a battle. A battle between the version of yourself that the world has imposed upon you and the version of yourself that you are fighting to reclaim.

## The Power of Self-Narrative

Every identity is built upon a foundation of stories—some inherited, some learned, and some forcibly assigned. These narratives are often established long before we ever realize they are shaping our reality. Think about the messages you absorbed in childhood. Maybe it was a teacher who dismissed your potential, a parent who unknowingly projected their fears onto you, or a society that categorized you based on circumstances beyond your control.

Psychologist Carl Rogers once said, *"The curious paradox is that when I accept myself just as I am, then I can change."* But for many, self-acceptance has been made nearly impossible by external narratives that reinforce the idea that they are broken, unworthy, or undeserving of redemption.

For most of my life, no amount of success could silence the inner voice that insisted, *"You're a fraud."* It didn't matter how much I accomplished—the fear of being "found out" as someone unworthy loomed over every achievement, and my brain followed suit ensuring I became that which I believed through self-sabotaging patterns. It was an inherited script, shaped by past fears and reinforced by fear-based labels. When I finally confronted that narrative, I realized that my struggle wasn't with the external world alone—it was with the identity I had unknowingly internalized.

The truth is, the greatest barriers we face are not always the physical ones. They are the unseen chains of identity—chains we were never meant to wear but have been burdened with nonetheless.

## Rewriting Your Story

Transformation doesn't begin with external change; it begins with internal reconstruction. It's not about pretending past failures never happened or erasing the scars of hardship. It's about reclaiming ownership of your story and choosing to see yourself through the lens of growth and resilience rather than limitation.

Imagine your life as a book where you are both the author and the protagonist. Up until now, you may have been living according to a script written by other people—society, family, past mistakes, systemic oppression. But that script is not permanent. Every page that follows is yours to rewrite.

Start by identifying the subconscious scripts running in the background. Write them down. Examine them. Challenge them. Ask yourself: *Who told me this was true?* Was it an experience? A person? A system that benefits from keeping me small?

Then, consciously reframe those beliefs. Instead of *"I always fail,"* reprogram it into *"I learn and grow from every challenge."* Instead of *"I don't belong,"* shift it to *"I bring unique value to every space I enter."* This isn't self-delusion—it's self-liberation. The words you repeat to yourself become the architecture of your identity.

## Real-World Resilience: Elizabeth Smart's Journey Beyond Victimhood

Elizabeth Smart was only fourteen years old when she was kidnapped from her Salt Lake City home. For nine traumatic months, Elizabeth endured unimaginable suffering and victimization. After she was rescued, many believed the trauma would define her life forever—that she'd always carry the identity of a victim. But Elizabeth made a powerful choice: she refused to remain emotionally trapped by her ordeal.

Determined to reclaim her life and identity, Elizabeth confronted the subconscious beliefs that kept her feeling powerless and hopeless. She committed to rebuilding her self-worth, stepping away from victimhood, and stepping into advocacy. Today, Elizabeth is a fierce advocate for survivors of abuse, a bestselling author, and an inspirational speaker. Her story shows us clearly that no matter what emotional trap we feel stuck in, we have the power to break free and rewrite our story.

Elizabeth Smart's resilience reveals that our past does not have to dictate our future. Let's explore exactly how you can begin reclaiming your own power and break free from the subconscious cycles holding you back.

## Harnessing Neuroplasticity for Transformation

Neuroplasticity is the brain's remarkable ability to change and adapt throughout life. This concept is crucial for individuals recovering from trauma or facing systemic barriers, as it offers a powerful tool for rewriting negative patterns and beliefs.

To apply neuroplasticity in your own life, start by recognizing the patterns you want to change. This could be a fear of failure, a tendency to self-sabotage, or a belief that success is unattainable. Once you've identified these patterns, begin to challenge them with new experiences and thoughts.

Here's a simple exercise to get started:

1. **Identify a Negative Pattern:** Choose one negative belief or behavior you want to change.

2. **Challenge It:** Write down three reasons why this belief is not true or why this behavior is holding you back.

3. **Replace It:** Create a new, positive affirmation to replace the old pattern. Repeat this affirmation daily.

4. **Practice Consistency:** Engage in activities that reinforce this new mindset regularly.

The same brain that has been conditioned by trauma, self-doubt, and failure is also the brain that can rebuild itself into a foundation for resilience, confidence, and achievement. By harnessing the power of neuroplasticity, you can begin to break free from the cycles that have held you back and start building a new, empowered life. We'll delve deeper into neuroplasticity in Chapter 2.

## 1.2 The Science of Breaking Free from Self-Sabotage

When you've spent years in survival mode, failure can become a twisted kind of refuge. It's not that you want to keep losing—it's that losing is familiar. The disappointment, the setbacks, the self-doubt—it's all part of a cycle that, at some point, your brain started accepting as the default. It may seem like self-sabotage is a personal flaw, but in reality, it's a deeply ingrained neurological process.

For those who have endured systemic barriers—whether it be the revolving door of the criminal justice system, generational poverty, or trauma that rewired the brain for survival rather than success—self-sabotage is often not a conscious choice. It's a program running in the background, dictating behaviors before you even realize what's happening. But like any program, it can be rewritten.

### The "Failure Loop" – How the Brain Gets Addicted to Failure

Imagine failure not as a single event, but as a loop—a self-reinforcing cycle embedded into your neural circuitry. Every time you stumble, your brain doesn't just register the mistake; it logs it, stores it, and primes you to expect the same outcome again. Over time, failure stops feeling like an accident and starts feeling like an inevitability.

For those who have faced repeated setbacks—rejections from jobs due to a criminal record, economic hardship that keeps opportunities just out of reach, or social stigma that closes doors before you even knock—the failure loop can feel inescapable. But it's not just external circumstances trapping you—it's the way your brain has been trained to respond to those circumstances.

Each time failure happens, your brain releases stress hormones like cortisol, reinforcing the association between setbacks and emotional distress. Eventually, the brain stops distinguishing between external failure and internal expectation. You don't just experience failure—you begin to *expect* it.

## The Comfort of the Known

It sounds counterintuitive, but your brain finds comfort in familiarity—even when that familiarity is pain. Psychologists call this *cognitive consistency,* the tendency of the mind to gravitate toward what it knows, even if it's destructive. This is why people often stay in toxic relationships, remain stuck in cycles of poverty, or keep making choices that lead to the same dead-end results.

I once had a conversation with a man who had spent over a decade in prison. After release, he tried to integrate into society, but every job rejection, every wary glance, every moment of exclusion reinforced the idea that he *belonged* in the system he was trying to escape. One night, facing homelessness and hopelessness, he committed a petty crime—*not because he wanted to go back to prison, but because prison was the only place he knew how to exist.*

This is the terrifying power of the failure loop. When the alternative—success, stability, self-worth—feels foreign, the brain clings to what is familiar. As Albert Ellis, the founder of Rational Emotive Behavior Therapy, put it: *"People don't just resist change. They resist loss."* And for many, losing the identity of struggle means stepping into an uncertain future.

## A Vicious Reinforcement

The most dangerous part of the failure loop isn't just how it makes you feel— it's how it shapes your identity. Every failure, every rejection, every moment of self-doubt gets internalized as proof that *this is who you are.* And the more you believe it, the more your brain ensures that belief plays out in reality.

This is why "just trying harder" doesn't work. You can't break free from self-sabotage through sheer willpower alone. You have to rewire your brain. You have to retrain it to expect *something different.*

And that starts with recognizing that failure is not a reflection of who you are. It's a pattern. And patterns can be broken.

The feeling of being trapped—whether by past failures, systemic barriers, or the weight of your own mind—is one of the most suffocating human experiences. It convinces you that no matter how hard you try, you'll always end up in the same place, reliving the same disappointments. But that belief? It's a lie. Not because hope is some blind, empty promise, but because science confirms that your brain—your *actual* neural wiring—can be changed. Your mind is not a prison with unbreakable walls; it's a living, breathing network of pathways that can be rewired, restructured, and reprogrammed for success.

## From Negative to Positive Pathways

Every choice you make—whether it's dwelling in self-doubt or actively shifting your mindset—has a physical impact on your brain. When you consciously disrupt old, negative thought patterns, you are actively forging new neural connections. Over time, these new pathways can override the destructive ones, just like how a new habit can replace an old one.

Think of your mind as a field overrun with weeds. Those weeds—the patterns of self-sabotage, fear, and limiting beliefs—have grown thick from years of reinforcement. At first, planting new, empowering beliefs may feel like a slow, frustrating process. But with every intentional thought, every conscious redirection, you are cultivating a new landscape. The weeds don't disappear overnight, but with consistency, they begin to wither, making room for something stronger to grow in their place.

Each time you replace *I'm not good enough* with *I am capable of learning and growing*, you strengthen new neural pathways. Each time you take action despite fear, your brain rewires itself to expect success rather than failure.

This is not some abstract concept—it's biology. And the more you work with it, the more it works for you.

## Practical Brain Exercises to Disrupt Negative Patterns

Understanding how the brain reinforces failure is one thing. Breaking the cycle is another. Theoretical knowledge without action is like a map without movement—it shows you where to go, but it won't get you there. True transformation requires deliberate, consistent effort to interrupt the patterns of self-sabotage and replace them with success-driven habits.

These exercises aren't just feel-good strategies; they are grounded in neuroscience and psychology, designed to rewire your brain at a fundamental level. Whether you've been conditioned by trauma, systemic barriers, or cycles of self-doubt, these techniques give you the tools to reclaim control over your mind and, ultimately, your life.

Here's how you can apply this understanding to break free from self-sabotage:

1. **Identify Your Triggers:** Start by recognizing situations or emotions that trigger self-sabotaging behaviors. This could be anything from procrastination to self-doubt.

2. **Challenge Negative Beliefs:** Once you've identified your triggers, challenge the underlying beliefs that drive them. Ask yourself if these beliefs are based on reality or past experiences that no longer apply.

3. **Replace Old Patterns with New Ones:** Intentionally replace old patterns with new, positive ones. This might involve creating a daily routine that reinforces success-oriented behaviors.

4. **Practice Consistency:** Consistency is crucial in rewiring your brain. Engage in activities that support your new mindset regularly, even if it feels unnatural at first.

By applying these strategies, you can begin to break the cycle of self-sabotage and move towards a more empowered, self-directed life. At the end of this chapter, you'll find a structured action plan you can use to integrate these new techniques.

## 1.3 The Emotional Traps Keeping You Stuck

Emotions are the invisible forces shaping our decisions, reactions, and ultimately, our destiny. They dictate how we interpret setbacks, whether we take action or retreat, and how we define ourselves in the face of hardship. When left unchecked, emotions can act as chains, binding us to past failures, paralyzing us with doubt, and distorting our perceptions of both success and failure.

For those who are in a time of rebuilding and recovery, these emotional traps are even more insidious. They are reinforced not just by personal experiences but by external forces that tell us we are unworthy of rising above our circumstances. But recognizing these emotional patterns is the first step to breaking free from them.

To break free from these emotional traps, you need to understand how they operate. Here are some common emotional traps and how to overcome them:

1. **Fear of Failure:** This fear often stems from past experiences where failure led to negative consequences. However, it can also prevent you from taking necessary risks to succeed. To overcome it, challenge the belief that failure is catastrophic. Instead, view it as a learning opportunity. Understand that success is also a significant point of fear and needs to be addressed.

2. **Guilt and Shame:** These emotions can stem from past traumas or mistakes. They can make you feel unworthy of success, causing self-sabotage. Recognize that guilt and shame are not objective truths but rather emotional responses that can be healed through self-forgiveness and acceptance.

3. **Anger and Resentment:** These emotions can fuel determination but also lead to burnout and stagnation if not managed. Channel anger into constructive action by setting clear goals and working towards them.

4. **Self-Pity:** This emotional trap can make you feel helpless, reinforcing a victim mindset. Break free by focusing on what you can control and taking small, consistent actions towards change.

Let's delve deeper into each of these traps and explore how they can be overcome:

### 1. Fear of Failure: The Paralyzing Script

Fear of failure is one of the most common emotional traps. It's the voice that tells you, "You'll never make it," or "You're not good enough." This fear is often rooted in past experiences where failure had severe consequences. For someone with a criminal record, the fear might be about being rejected by society again. For those who have faced financial devastation, it might be about losing everything once more.

To break this trap, you need to reframe your perception of failure. Instead of seeing it as a permanent setback, view it as a stepping stone to success. Thomas Edison, the inventor of the light bulb, is famously quoted as saying, "I have not failed. I've just found 10,000 ways that won't work." This mindset shift can help you see failure not as an end but as a part of the journey.

**If you're struggling with a similar fear, here are some steps you can take:**

1. **Identify Your Fears:** Start by recognizing the fears that hold you back. Is it fear of failure, fear of success, or something else?

2. **Challenge Negative Beliefs:** Once you've identified your fears, challenge the underlying beliefs that drive them. Ask yourself if these beliefs are based on reality or past experiences that no longer apply.

3. **Practice Self-Forgiveness:** Recognize that past mistakes are not defining characteristics. Practice self-forgiveness and focus on moving forward.

4. **Build a Support Network:** Surround yourself with people who support and believe in your potential.

## 2. Guilt and Shame: The Weight of the Past

Guilt and regret are some of the heaviest emotional burdens a person can carry. They don't just remind you of past mistakes—they chain you to them, whispering that you are irredeemable, that your failures define you. If you have ever been marked by a past you cannot change—whether it's a conviction, a broken relationship, or a moment of weakness that altered the trajectory of your life—then you know how suffocating these emotions can be.

But here's the truth: your mistakes are not the sum total of who you are. They are not the final sentence in the story of your life. The key to breaking free from guilt and regret isn't in pretending these emotions don't exist—it's in transforming them into fuel for growth, resilience, and renewal.

### Reclaiming Your Narrative

Guilt and regret, when left unchecked, become the authors of your life story. They turn every page into a reflection of what you *should* have done, what you *could* have avoided, how things *might* have been different. But you do not have to let them control the pen.

Your past is not an indefinite prison sentence—it is a chapter. Every person has made mistakes, but not everyone chooses to be defined by them. *Mel Robbins* puts it bluntly: *"You're not your mistakes. You are the lessons learned from those mistakes."*

I know what it feels like to wake up every day with a past that won't let you go. For years, I replayed every misstep, every missed opportunity, every wrong decision like a broken record in my mind. Guilt and shame crushed my spirit. I had no desire to continue in a life that felt hopeless, especially after causing so much unintended harm to everyone around me. It took years of therapy and I continued even after I was no longer court-ordered to attend. I still had so much unresolved personal regret. It wasn't until I started reframing my past and separating myself from my thoughts—viewing it as a source of knowledge rather than shame—that I was able to start moving forward.

## Actionable Shifts for Moving Forward

Breaking free from guilt and regret is not a passive process. It requires action, intentional and repeated, to reshape the way you see yourself and your past.

- **Daily Reflection Journal:** Write down one regret each day—but instead of dwelling on what went wrong, write the lesson you've taken from it. Over time, you will start to see your past not as a series of failures, but as a guidebook of wisdom.

- **Create a Personal Mantra:** The words you tell yourself matter. Choose a phrase that reinforces your growth—something like, "I am not defined by my past; I am empowered by my lessons." Repeat this to yourself whenever guilt tries to creep in.

- **Surround Yourself with Growth-Oriented People:** Guilt thrives in isolation. Connect with those who see your potential rather than your past. Whether it's through support groups, personal development workshops, or simply spending time with people who uplift you, make sure your environment encourages growth.

- **Seek Professional Guidance if Needed:** Some wounds are too deep to heal alone. If guilt or regret is consuming your mental and emotional energy, seeking therapy or counseling can provide a structured way to process and release these feelings. If you are court-ordered for therapy, make the deliberate and conscious decision to use this time for self-discovery. It's not a punishment, it's an opportunity!

The past *cannot* be changed. But your relationship with it can. When you take active steps to shift your perspective—when you choose forgiveness over shame, learning over regret—you reclaim control over your life.

You are not your worst mistake. You are the person who rises from it.

### 3. Anger and Resentment: The Fuel for Change

Anger and resentment can be powerful motivators, but they can also lead to burnout and stagnation if not managed properly. These emotions often arise from feelings of injustice or betrayal. For those who have faced systemic barriers, anger can be a natural response to the unfairness of their situation.

To channel anger into constructive action, set clear goals and work towards them. Use your anger as fuel to drive change, whether it's advocating for justice or building a better life for yourself. Remember, anger is not the problem; it's how you choose to express it that matters.

### Embracing Forgiveness

Forgiveness is not about erasing the past. It is not about excusing what happened or pretending that mistakes don't have consequences. *Forgiveness is about reclaiming your power from the things that hold you hostage.*

Many people think they need to be "ready" to forgive themselves or others— that one day they will wake up and the resentment will simply fade away. But forgiveness is not a feeling. It is a *decision*. And it is one that you must make over and over again.

*Dr. Fred Luskin,* a leading researcher on forgiveness, found that people who actively practice forgiveness experience lower stress, improved mental health, and even better physical well-being. But more importantly, they experience *freedom*—freedom from the toxic loop of self-recrimination that keeps them stuck.

One simple way to integrate forgiveness into your daily life is through a brief reflection practice. Every night before bed, take five minutes to acknowledge anything from the day that you need to release—whether it's self-blame, resentment toward someone else, or lingering regret. Write it down, and as you do, make the choice to let it go.

### 4. Self-Pity: The Victim Mindset

Self-pity is an emotional trap that can make you feel helpless, reinforcing a victim mindset. It's the voice that says, "I'll never make it," or "Life is unfair." This mindset keeps you stuck in a cycle of dependency on external circumstances for change.

To break free from self-pity, focus on what you can control. Take small, consistent actions towards change. Celebrate your successes, no matter how small they may seem. By doing so, you begin to shift from a victim to a leader mindset, taking ownership of your life and your future. You will move away from self-pity towards self-compassion.

## Owning Your Decisions

Every decision you make—no matter how small—shapes the trajectory of your life. Imagine that each choice is a brushstroke on the canvas of your future. You can't erase past mistakes, but you *can* create a masterpiece moving forward.

My public moral failure left me dejected and despondent. I found slight solace in fleeting thoughts of blame, but every attempt to defend myself and my actions only led right back to me. I learned to ask myself without judgement: *What could I have done differently?* Then, I would visualize myself making different choices. I cultivated compassion for the version of myself that did the best I could in that moment, but learned to give this new version of me a different choice and outcome. That mindset shift changed everything. Rather than staying stuck in self-pity, I used the failure as a lesson, applied what I learned, and slowly rebuilt credibility with myself, knowing I will never cause harm like that ever again.

Taking responsibility isn't about self-blame—it's about empowerment. It's the moment you stop seeing yourself as a product of your past and start recognizing yourself as the architect of your future.

## Embracing Accountability

Life is full of unexpected challenges. You can't control the biases of others, the obstacles in your path, or the unfairness of the world. However, what you can control is how you respond to these challenges. This is where accountability comes in—taking ownership of your actions and choices, even in the face of adversity.

Imagine two ships caught in a storm. One drifts aimlessly, at the mercy of the waves, while the other has a captain who adjusts the sails, adapts to the winds, and steers the ship through the chaos. The latter is what accountability looks like—refusing to let external circumstances dictate your journey.

I've experienced this firsthand. The legal system handed me a label that felt like a permanent scarlet letter, forever branding me in the eyes of others. The narrative online was misleading and damaging, with no clear way to set the record straight. The damage was done, and I faced a choice: blame the unfairness of it all or take control of the one thing I could—my response.

It took years of healing in therapy while on probation, but I finally chose to take control. I sought mentorship, with a new healthy mindset toward it, expanded my skill set, and aligned myself with people who challenged me to use my circumstances as an opportunity to encourage others. Slowly but surely, I found my way out of the storm. Accountability isn't just about owning your past; it's about choosing your next steps with clarity and purpose.

**To apply this principle in your own life, consider the following:**

1. **Recognize What You Can Control:** In any situation, identify what is within your power to change or influence.

2. **Take Ownership:** Acknowledge your role in the situation and take responsibility for your actions.

3. **Seek Support:** Surround yourself with mentors or peers who encourage and challenge you to grow.

4. **Plan Your Next Steps:** With clarity and purpose, decide how you will move forward, adapting to challenges as they arise.

## The Power of Radical Self-Compassion

Radical self-compassion is a revolutionary act in a world that conditions us to be our own harshest critics. It is not indulgence, nor is it an excuse to avoid accountability. Instead, it is a shift in perspective—one that transforms relentless self-judgment into a foundation for resilience, growth, and self-worth. It is the act of treating yourself with the same grace and understanding that you would offer a friend who is struggling.

Society has a way of reinforcing the idea that some people deserve redemption while others do not. Self-compassion is often the last thing we feel entitled to. But what if we reject that notion? What if we reclaim the right to see ourselves through a lens of understanding rather than condemnation? This is the essence of radical self-compassion: the refusal to see yourself as unworthy of healing.

One powerful approach is mindful self-compassion meditation. This practice involves setting aside 10–15 minutes a day to observe your thoughts without judgment. Instead of spiraling into self-criticism, you learn to acknowledge your pain with acceptance and curiosity.

Learn to observe your thoughts as if they were passing clouds. I love clouds. Freely floating along, changing shape as they go, providing shade from the harsh rays of sunlight. The judgment will lose its grip on you the more you separate yourself from your thoughts through mindfulness. This shift in self-treatment is more than a personal comfort; it is a radical act of defiance against every societal force that has told you that you are not enough. By treating yourself with dignity instead of pity, you dismantle the narratives that have kept you imprisoned in shame and self-doubt.

Research supports this transformation. Studies have shown that mindfulness-based self-compassion lowers cortisol (the stress hormone) while increasing oxytocin, the chemical linked to feelings of safety and connection. This rewiring of the brain makes it easier to replace self-recrimination with a sense of inner security.

Another powerful tool is compassionate letter writing. This involves writing a letter to yourself as if you were comforting a friend. You acknowledge your struggles, validate your pain, and remind yourself of your worth. The act of externalizing these words, of seeing them written in your own hand, can be profoundly healing.

I have kept letters I've written to myself during some of the darkest moments of my life. Letters that say, *You are not beyond redemption. You are not defined by this pain.* And when self-doubt creeps back in, I read them. They remind me that I have already walked through fire—and survived.

The key is to make self-compassion a habit.

1. **Notice self-criticism in real time. When you catch yourself being self-critical, ask:** Would I say this to a friend? If not, reframe the thought.

2. Create a self-compassion mantra. Something simple like, "I am doing the best I can, and that is enough," can serve as a lifeline in difficult moments.

3. Keep a self-compassion journal. Write down daily examples of how you showed yourself kindness or moments when you challenged negative self-talk.

4. Surround yourself with supportive voices. If your environment reinforces self-doubt, find people—mentors, friends, therapists—who encourage self-acceptance.

Every time you choose self-compassion, you are rewriting the script. You are choosing to rise.

## 1.4 Shifting from Victim to Leader Mindset

The journey to breaking cycles of failure begins with a fundamental shift in mindset—from seeing yourself as a victim to embracing the role of a leader. This transformation isn't about ignoring past injustices or traumas; it's about recognizing that you have the power to redefine your future.

A victim mindset often stems from experiences where you felt powerless or trapped. It can manifest as self-pity, blame, or a sense of helplessness.

However, this mindset keeps you stuck in a cycle of dependency on external circumstances for change.

In contrast, a leader mindset is about taking responsibility for your life. It involves recognizing that you have the power to make choices, to challenge negative beliefs, and to create the life you want. This mindset doesn't deny the past but uses it as a foundation for growth.

**Here's how you can begin to shift from a victim to a leader mindset:**

1. **Acknowledge Your Past:** Recognize the injustices or traumas you've faced, but avoid letting them define your present or future.

2. **Identify Your Strengths:** Focus on the strengths and resilience that have helped you survive difficult situations.

3. **Set Clear Goals:** Define what you want to achieve and create a plan to get there. This helps you move from a reactive to a proactive stance.

4. **Practice Self-Responsibility:** Take ownership of your actions and decisions. Instead of blaming external circumstances, focus on what you can control.

5. **Surround Yourself with Support:** Build a network of people who support and believe in your potential.

## A New Narrative

We have all been victimized at some point in our lives, and we have all caused harm. Releasing the victim mindset means rewriting your internal script. It's a conscious decision to stop seeing yourself as someone life *happens* to and start seeing yourself as someone who *creates* life on their own terms.

When I discarded the old narrative that had kept me stuck for years, the one that told me I was undeserving of success, the one that whispered I would never be anything more than my past mistakes, I was set free. That story was comfortable—but it was also a lie.

So, I wrote a new one. One where I wasn't a casualty of my circumstances, but a strategist who used every experience—good or bad—as raw material for growth. One where setbacks weren't proof of failure, but evidence of resilience.

You have the same power.

Let go of the outdated narrative that tells you who you *should* be based on your past. Start writing a new one—one where you reclaim your agency, transform your challenges into strengths, and lead yourself toward the life you deserve.

Because here's the truth: You are not a victim. You are not an offender. You are the author of your own story.

## Building Forward Momentum

Setbacks are not roadblocks; they are recalibrations. When harnessed correctly, they propel you forward. The challenge is to resist the instinct to stop moving. Each moment of adversity offers an opportunity to gain insight, refine your approach, and build momentum.

I once met a man who had been fired from every job he was able to secure after leaving the criminal justice system. He would disclose his background in good faith, be offered a job based on his skills, only to have an employee or customer discover his label and put pressure on the owner to fire him. This happened every time. The weight of rejection was crushing, but instead of resigning himself to a life of doors closed in his face, he began using every rejection as data. He focused on self-discovery, forged new connections and relationships and even launched a side business while continuing his search. Over time, his relentless persistence transformed his circumstances—he landed a leadership role in a field that had once dismissed him outright. His setbacks had not buried him; they had *built him*.

This is the essence of *turning failure into fuel*. Every time you extract a lesson, every time you analyze and adjust, you create movement in the right direction. No setback is wasted if it teaches you something. No rejection is final if you refuse to let it be.

So, as you move forward, ask yourself: *What is this setback trying to teach me?* What insight can I pull from this experience that will serve me later? The answers to these questions are the blueprints for your next steps.

Because setbacks are not signs that you should stop. *They are evidence that you are still moving forward.*

## Embracing Continuous Learning

The ability to view challenges as learning experiences is what separates those who stagnate from those who thrive. Imagine standing at the base of a mountain. A *fixed mindset* sees the peak as unreachable, believing that if you weren't naturally equipped to climb, you never will be. A *growth mindset*, however, sees a different reality: the mountain is scalable with the right strategy, persistence, and willingness to adapt along the way.

When you are incarcerated or on probation/parole, the sentence you are given feels like that proverbial mountain. It's hard to even imagine reaching the top, let alone seeing life from the perspective of the other side. Especially when you feel like any misstep will land you back at the bottom. But in time, each milestone is an opportunity to reflect and see how far you have already climbed. You are stronger than you think, gathering new tools along the way reinforcing your own internal belief that you will make it.

This approach wasn't just a coping mechanism—it was a turning point. By treating failure as a *feedback loop* rather than a dead end, I began to see my sentence for what it was: an invitation to learn. Research in positive psychology confirms that individuals who approach challenges with curiosity rather than fear are more likely to innovate, adapt, and ultimately succeed. When you shift your perspective, obstacles become stepping stones, and every hardship becomes part of your education.

## The Power of Storytelling

One of the most powerful tools in shifting from a victim to a leader mindset is storytelling. The stories we tell ourselves about our past, present, and future shape our identity and influence our actions. When you're trapped in a victim mindset, your story often revolves around what has been done to you. However, when you shift to a leader mindset, your story becomes about what you can achieve and how you can use your experiences to empower others.

Think about how you can reframe your own story:

- **From Victim to Survivor:** Instead of focusing on what happened to you, focus on how you survived and what strengths you developed during those times.

- **From Survivor to Leader:** Use your experiences to inspire and guide others. Share your story as a testament to resilience and transformation.

By adopting a leader mindset, you begin to break free from the cycles that have held you back. You start to see challenges as opportunities for growth rather than threats to your well-being. This mindset is not about ignoring the past but about using it to empower your future.

# Chapter 1 Case Study: Jay Jordan

## Background:

Jay Jordan grew up in Stockton, California, during the era of the 1994 Clinton Crime Bill, which led to increased incarceration rates. At 18, he was arrested for vehicle theft and subsequently served a seven-year prison sentence. During his incarceration, Jordan faced the harsh realities of the criminal justice system, including time in solitary confinement.

## Application of Principles:

- **Identifying and Rewriting Subconscious Scripts:** Jordan recognized that his environment and past experiences had ingrained limiting beliefs and behaviors. He made a conscious effort to challenge and change these internal narratives, understanding that to break the cycle of self-sabotage, he needed to transform his mindset.

- **Confronting Emotional Traps:** He acknowledged the emotional patterns that led to destructive decisions. By addressing feelings of hopelessness and anger, Jordan worked towards emotional healing, which was crucial in preventing relapse into old behaviors.

- **Breaking the Cycle of Self-Sabotage:** Post-incarceration, Jordan faced numerous barriers due to his criminal record, which hindered employment opportunities and societal reintegration. Instead of succumbing to these challenges, he used them as motivation to advocate for systemic change, thereby breaking the cycle not just for himself but for others in similar situations.

## Outcome:

After his release, Jay Jordan became a prominent activist and leader in criminal justice reform. He served as the director of the Second Chance Project with Californians for Safety and Justice, focusing on policies to assist former inmates in reintegrating into society. In 2022, he played a pivotal role in advocating for California's Assembly Bill 1076, aimed at automating the expungement of eligible arrest and conviction records, thereby removing significant barriers to employment and housing for millions. Jordan's journey from incarceration to becoming the CEO of the Alliance for Safety and Justice exemplifies the power of breaking negative cycles and transforming one's life through conscious effort and resilience.

## 1.5 The First Action Plan – Reset Your Mindset

### 1.5 The First Action Plan - Reset Your Mindset

Now that you've begun to understand the hidden mindset programming and emotional traps holding you back, it's time to take action. The following plan is designed to help you reset your mindset and start breaking free from the cycles of failure.

## Craft Your Reset Statement

This is your declaration of intent. A promise to yourself that your past no longer defines you. A statement that, from this moment forward, you are choosing something different.

It might look like this:

*"I am done letting my past define me. I choose to learn, grow, and build a future filled with purpose."*

Or this:

*"I am not the sum of my mistakes. I am the architect of my future, and I reclaim my power starting now."*

Whatever words you choose, make them powerful. Make them personal. And write them somewhere you will see them often.

## Daily Mindset Reset Plan

1. **Morning Reflection (10 minutes):**

   - Start each day by journaling your thoughts and emotions. Identify any negative patterns or self-doubt that arise.

   - Challenge these thoughts by reframing them in a positive light. For example, instead of "I'll never succeed," say "I am capable of achieving my goals."

2. **Mindfulness Practice (15 minutes):**

   - Engage in a mindfulness exercise, such as meditation or deep breathing, to become more aware of your subconscious thoughts.

   - Use this time to focus on the present moment and let go of past regrets or future anxieties.

3. **Gratitude Exercise (5 minutes):**

   - Write down three things you are grateful for each day. This helps shift your focus from what's lacking to what you already have.

   - Reflect on how these things positively impact your life and mindset.

4. **Evening Review (10 minutes):**

   - Before bed, review your day. Identify moments where you successfully challenged negative thoughts or behaviors.

   - Celebrate these small victories and plan how you can build on them tomorrow.

## Weekly Challenge

- **Identify and Challenge One Negative Belief:** Choose one negative belief that holds you back and challenge it throughout the week. Replace it with a positive affirmation and repeat it daily.

- **Share Your Progress:** Share your progress with a trusted friend or mentor. This can help keep you accountable and motivated.

## Monthly Reflection

- **Assess Your Progress:** Take time to reflect on how far you've come. Identify areas where you've improved and where you still need to work.

- **Adjust Your Plan:** Based on your reflections, adjust your daily and weekly practices to better align with your goals.

By following this action plan, you'll begin to reset your mindset, breaking free from the cycles that have held you back. Remember, transformation is a journey, and every small step counts.

The first time I wrote my reset statement, it felt strange—like I was making a promise I wasn't yet sure I could keep. But as I read it, day after day, something shifted. It became a mantra. A contract with myself. A daily reminder that no matter how much I had lost, I still had control over what happened next.

This statement is your North Star. The first anchor of your new mindset. And every time you revisit it, let it remind you: you are in control now.

## Chapter 1 Summary: Breaking the Cycle

You've taken the first step toward true transformation by exposing the hidden mindset programming that has shaped your life. The beliefs and habits ingrained in your subconscious—many of which formed without your awareness—have been dictating your actions, keeping you stuck in cycles of self-sabotage, fear, and doubt.

But now, you see the truth: your past does not define your future.

In this chapter, you've uncovered how deeply embedded subconscious programming, past experiences, and systemic barriers influence up to 95% of your daily choices. You've also learned that breaking free from destructive cycles starts with recognizing these invisible scripts and rewriting them with intentional action.

The next step? Rewiring your brain for lasting success.

In Chapter 2, you'll dive into the neuroscience of transformation—learning how to reprogram your brain using neuroplasticity, mental rehearsal, and practical brain-hacking techniques. You'll also confront the emotional traps that keep you stuck—like fear of failure and guilt—and gain strategies to break through them.

With this foundation in place, you are ready to take back control of your mindset, rewrite your story, and start living life on your terms.

# Chapter 2

# Rewiring Your Brain for Success – The Neuroscience of Transformation

*"Believe you can and you're halfway there."* – Theodore Roosevelt

In Chapter 1, we explored how hidden mindset programming can keep you stuck in cycles of failure. Now, it's time to delve into the science behind transforming your mind and breaking free from those cycles. Did you know that every thought physically changes your brain? This means success is not some distant dream—it's a program you can install directly into your neural pathways.

There's a quiet revolution happening inside our heads every single day. While we often consider our thoughts as ephemeral whispers, modern neuroscience reveals they are, in fact, the architects of our reality. In this chapter, we dive deep into the mechanisms that allow our brains to change, adapt, and ultimately support the success we envision. In this chapter we'll explore how the power of thought creates our world, dissect the marvel of neuroplasticity, and uncover why practices like mental rehearsal aren't just feel-good techniques but essential strategies for genuine transformation.

## Preview – Meet Shaka Senghor

What if your worst decision defined you forever? Shaka Senghor once believed it would. Convicted at 19 for murder, sentenced to 19 years, including 7 years in solitary confinement, he could have easily given up on himself. But Shaka discovered a powerful truth: we all have the ability to rewire our minds. His remarkable transformation demonstrates the potential we all carry within—waiting to be awakened.

You'll discover Shaka's full journey at the end of this chapter and see precisely how he rewired his mind for success.

# 2.1 The Power of Thought – How Your Brain Creates Reality

Our thoughts are more than just fleeting ideas—they are dynamic forces that shape our lives. The old adage "as a man thinks, so is he" resonates with a profound truth: each thought is a building block of our reality. In this section, we examine how the brain constructs our experience, starting with the groundbreaking concept of neuroplasticity, then uncovering the transformative role of mental rehearsal, and finally, learning how to align thoughts, emotions, and actions into a cohesive force for change.

## Neuroplasticity Explained – Your Brain Can Rewire Itself at Any Age

Imagine your brain not as a static map of predetermined routes but as a vibrant, ever-evolving metropolis—a city where new roads are built, old ones are renovated, and obsolete pathways are gradually replaced. This is neuroplasticity in action: the brain's remarkable capacity to reorganize its structure and function in response to new experiences.

## Transformative Flexibility

For decades, it was widely believed that our brains became fixed after a certain age, that the neural architecture of adulthood was immutable. Today, research by pioneers such as Dr. Michael Merzenich has shattered that myth. Modern neuroscience shows that our brains remain flexible throughout our lives. This transformative flexibility means that every new skill you learn or every fresh idea you entertain can forge new neural connections, effectively rewriting the script of your mind. Think of it as updating the software of your brain—each deliberate action or thought is a small line of code that, over time, transforms your cognitive landscape into one optimized for growth and adaptation.

## Evidence in Everyday Life

Neuroplasticity is not confined to the realm of clinical research; it's a phenomenon at work in your daily routine. Whether you're learning a new language, mastering a musical instrument, or simply adopting a different way of thinking about your challenges, you are actively engaging in neural remodeling. As Norman Doidge famously stated, "The brain is a highly adaptive organ," and every experience you have contributes to that adaptation. Have you ever thought about the countless individuals who, through persistent effort, who learned to overcome neurological setbacks after a stroke, or those who have reinvented themselves in later stages of life? These real-world examples serve as a vivid reminder that our neural circuits are continuously in flux, sculpted by our ongoing interactions with the world.

## Real-Life Rewiring

Picture someone returning to society after 15 years behind bars, overwhelmed by the technology, norms, and immediate dismissals from employers. It might feel hopeless at first, but every single time they choose to learn a new digital skill—despite fear or embarrassment—the brain builds fresh pathways, turning "I can't adapt" into "I am adapting." Ultimately, new roads form that support success.

## Why "Mental Rehearsal" Is Key to Success

Have you ever noticed that before a big game, athletes spend hours in the quiet solitude of their minds, visualizing every pass, every sprint, every moment of triumph? That's mental rehearsal at work—a powerful technique that harnesses your brain's ability to simulate experiences long before they unfold in reality. While this practice is a staple in the world of sports, its benefits extend far beyond the playing field; mental rehearsal is a critical tool for anyone aiming to achieve lasting change and peak performance in any area of life.

## The Science Behind the Practice

Neuroscientists have uncovered a fascinating truth: when you vividly imagine an action, your brain fires off many of the same neural circuits that it would if you were actually performing that action. This process is akin to a high-intensity training session for your mind. Dr. Joe Dispenza, a renowned expert in the field, captures this idea succinctly: "When you imagine, you create a new neural pathway that will eventually become your reality." In other words, mental rehearsal doesn't just prepare you for success—it actively molds the brain's architecture to support your ambitions.

Research has shown that this form of cognitive rehearsal can lead to significant improvements in performance. For instance, studies on musicians reveal that practicing a piece in their mind can improve their ability to play it, almost as effectively as physically rehearsing. This scientific validation underscores that mental rehearsal is not merely a fanciful daydream but a tangible method for enhancing your capabilities. Every time you mentally simulate a successful outcome, you reinforce the pathways necessary for that success, effectively training your brain to perform under pressure.

If you've spent years being told "You'll never break free from the stigma of your record," mental rehearsal helps replace that internal voice. Instead, you see yourself calmly addressing a potential employer's concerns, showcasing your resilience, and refusing to be shamed by the past.

## Real-World Resilience: Dr. Joe Dispenza's Journey of Healing

When Dr. Joe Dispenza was hit by a vehicle during a triathlon, doctors told him he might never walk again. Suffering from severe spinal injuries, his future seemed bleak. The recommended surgery promised little hope for recovery and lifelong chronic pain. Instead of accepting this fate, Joe decided to take his healing into his own hands—by literally rewiring his brain.

Drawing on his extensive knowledge of neuroscience, meditation, and visualization techniques, Joe spent weeks mentally rehearsing the reconstruction of his spine, visualizing every nerve, muscle, and vertebra healing itself. He committed fully to this daily mental practice, defying medical skepticism. Remarkably, within months, Joe was not only back on his feet but fully recovered, pain-free, and physically active once again.

Joe Dispenza's incredible recovery demonstrates the profound power our brains have when we actively rewire them for healing and success. Today, as an internationally acclaimed neuroscientist and bestselling author, he helps thousands tap into their brain's potential to transform their health, careers, and lives.

Dr. Dispenza's powerful example reveals how dramatically we can change our lives by intentionally rewiring our brains. Now, let's explore exactly how you can harness this same power to create your own path to success.

## Practical Application

Incorporating mental rehearsal into your daily routine doesn't require a dramatic overhaul of your schedule—it simply calls for a few dedicated minutes each day. Start by identifying a goal or challenge you're facing. Then, find a quiet space where you won't be interrupted. Close your eyes and begin to visualize the scenario in vivid detail. Imagine not just the final outcome but also the journey: the obstacles you'll overcome, the strategies you'll employ, and the skills you'll hone along the way.

For example, if you're preparing for an important meeting, picture yourself entering the room with poise, engaging confidently with colleagues, and articulating your ideas clearly. Focus on the sensations: the steady rhythm of your breath, the firmness of your handshake, the clarity in your voice. Over time, this practice of detailed visualization creates a sense of inevitability about your success. It's like running mental simulations that prime you for real-world execution.

Pairing this exercise with a simple breathing routine can amplify its effects. Inhale deeply as you picture success, and exhale slowly to release any lingering doubts. This method not only reinforces positive neural pathways but also anchors you in the present moment, readying you for the challenges ahead.

## How to Align Thoughts, Emotions, and Actions for Real Change

True transformation isn't just about thinking positive thoughts; it's about creating a seamless synergy between what you think, what you feel, and how you act. This alignment is the cornerstone of sustainable change and lasting success.

## The Triad of Transformation

Imagine your mind, heart, and body as the sections of an intricate orchestra. When each plays in perfect harmony, the resulting symphony is nothing short of transcendent. In the realm of personal development, aligning your thoughts with your emotions and actions creates a powerful feedback loop where every element reinforces the other. Renowned psychologist Daniel Goleman emphasizes that emotional intelligence—the capacity to manage and harness your emotions—is key to bridging the gap between cognitive intentions and practical outcomes. In essence, your thoughts (the mind), feelings (the heart), and behaviors (the body) must work in concert for genuine transformation to occur. This integrated approach not only fosters clarity but also ensures that every decision you make is deeply rooted in both reason and passion.

## Practical Steps to Achieve Alignment

Achieving alignment starts with a conscious examination of your inner dialogue. Begin by asking yourself: Are your thoughts fueling optimism, or are they breeding doubt? Notice how your emotions respond to these thoughts—do they uplift you or drag you down? To foster alignment, pair this introspection with emotional self-regulation techniques such as mindfulness or meditation. These practices allow you to observe your feelings without being overwhelmed by them, creating a mental space where your intentions and emotions can meet harmoniously.

Once you have achieved clarity in thought and emotion, translate this unified state into action. Design daily habits that mirror your aspirations. For instance, if you envision yourself as a successful entrepreneur, cultivate a routine that supports that identity. This might include networking with like-minded individuals, dedicating time to continuous learning, or simply maintaining a disciplined schedule that reinforces your goals. Over time, these deliberate actions become ingrained habits that sustain your vision, ensuring that your inner beliefs are consistently reflected in your external world.

## 2.2  Breaking the Habit of Being Your Old Self

Our minds often cling to the past like a well-worn garment, familiar and comforting even when it no longer serves us. This tendency is rooted in the brain's preference for efficiency and the path of least resistance. After years of negative reinforcement—such as constant rejections or the stigma tied to a criminal record—returning to old habits can feel safer than risking the pain of change.

Charles Duhigg once observed, "Habits are the invisible architecture of our daily lives." These ingrained routines become our default settings, even if they lead to outcomes we no longer desire. To break free from these habits, you need to cultivate awareness. Start by noticing when you slip into old patterns. Ask yourself: "Is this response serving the person I want to be, or is it a relic of who I once was?"

### Identifying and Eliminating Old Mental Programming

To break free from your past self, you must first identify the outdated mental programs that have been running silently in the background. These scripts, often installed during childhood or through systemic oppression, tell you "You'll never succeed" or "People like you aren't meant to flourish." They quietly dictate how you react to obstacles.

Think of your mind as a computer loaded with software that was installed long ago, often without your conscious consent. Over time, these programs become outdated, hindering your ability to upgrade to a more vibrant, capable version of yourself. When you become aware that a critical inner voice, echoing with self-doubt and negativity, is nothing more than an old program running on autopilot, you have taken the first step of separating yourself from your thoughts.

To identify these patterns, start by journaling your thoughts and tracking recurring themes of self-criticism or limitation. Look for patterns that point to an underlying script—perhaps a recurring belief that you're not worthy of success or that change is too risky. Once identified, challenge these patterns with evidence to the contrary. Cognitive-behavioral techniques, such as reframing negative thoughts, can be invaluable in this process.

## Building a New Identity That Matches the Person You Want to Become

Building a new identity is not about erasing your past; it's about reimagining it, extracting the lessons, and using them to craft a version of yourself that aligns with your highest aspirations. Let's think about the story of Malala Yousafzai, who was once labeled as a victim of oppression but chose to redefine herself as a global advocate for education. She took her experiences and used them to fuel her mission, becoming a symbol of resilience and courage.

To build a new identity, start by vividly envisioning the person you want to be. What qualities does this new identity embody? Confidence, resilience, creativity? Picture yourself living that life. This isn't mere daydreaming; it's a deliberate act of cognitive and emotional alignment.

Next, set small, manageable goals that reflect this envisioned self. If you aspire to be more assertive, practice speaking up in meetings or expressing your opinions in social settings. If creativity is a core trait of your new identity, carve out time each day for creative pursuits—be it writing, painting, or even brainstorming innovative ideas at work. Over time, these actions accumulate, gradually reprogramming your self-concept.

Embrace feedback and celebrate your progress. Surround yourself with people who reflect the qualities you admire. As you continue to align your behaviors with your new self-image, you'll find that the old mental programming begins to fade into the background, replaced by a vibrant, forward-looking identity that is entirely your own.

## 2.3 The Success Mindset Formula

Imagine a mindset so powerful that it becomes the very engine driving your achievements—a formula that transforms ordinary thought into extraordinary outcomes. In this section, we unravel the success mindset formula, revealing the three foundational beliefs that underpin the lives of highly successful people, outlining how you can install new empowering beliefs, and demonstrating how visualization and affirmations—grounded in neuroscience—can cement these changes into your reality.

### The 3 Foundational Beliefs of Highly Successful People

Successful individuals don't stumble upon greatness by accident; they cultivate it through a set of core beliefs that shape every decision, every action, and every moment of perseverance. These beliefs form the very bedrock upon which they build their lives, providing a framework that transforms challenges into opportunities and setbacks into catalysts for growth. Next, we will delve into the three foundational beliefs that have empowered some of the world's most accomplished individuals, exploring how these principles can be adopted to redefine your own path to success. Researchers find that truly successful individuals—whether they overcame extreme poverty or reentry from incarceration—share three beliefs: Belief in personal agency, growth mindset, and abundance.

### Belief in Personal Agency

At the heart of every remarkable achievement lies a steadfast conviction: you are the architect of your destiny. This belief in personal agency means understanding that every choice you make—whether it's a triumphant victory or a challenging setback—is within your control. It is a refusal to succumb to the notion that external circumstances dictate your fate. Instead, successful people recognize that they have the power to change themselves, regardless of the obstacles in their way.

When I decided to become an entrepreneur, I had weathered a series of early failures, each one threatening to extinguish my dreams. I hadn't cultivated a winning mindset yet, and was terrified of being "found out" if I put my name out there. As I started taking authorship of my own story, I began declared with unwavering resolve, "I am not defined by my circumstances—I define my circumstances." That moment encapsulated the essence of personal agency. It was a vivid reminder that true empowerment comes from taking responsibility for every facet of your life. When you own your decisions, you create a foundation for relentless growth. I was able to reframe how I looked at my seemingly early failures in business as evidence of old programming still at work undermining my own success, and pivot. I wasn't bad at business. I was programmed to sabotage myself. Studies in behavioral psychology suggest that individuals who embrace personal agency are more likely to persevere in the face of hardship, ultimately achieving higher levels of success and satisfaction.

## Belief in the Power of Growth

Embracing a growth mindset transforms the way you view obstacles. Instead of seeing challenges as insurmountable barriers, those with a growth mindset perceive them as opportunities to learn and improve. According to Carol Dweck's pioneering research, individuals who believe that their abilities can be developed are more resilient and successful than those who view talent as a fixed trait. In other words, failure isn't a dead end—it's an integral part of the journey toward mastery.

## Belief in Abundance

The third foundational belief that sets successful people apart is a profound trust in abundance. Rather than operating from a mindset of scarcity—where every achievement is viewed as a zero-sum game—they see the world as full of opportunities. This belief in abundance liberates them from the paralyzing fear of competition and fosters a spirit of collaboration. It's the conviction that the universe is generous, and that by contributing positively, you invite further prosperity into your life.

For example, imagine a collaborative project where the team's shared belief in abundance creates an atmosphere of mutual support and innovation. Rather than hoarding resources or ideas out of fear that someone else's success would diminish their own, each team member freely contributes, knowing that collective achievement only amplifies individual potential. This shift from a scarcity mentality to one of abundance not only will improve the project's outcomes but also can deepen the bonds within the team. This is hard when you've been negatively labeled, feel like you can't trust anyone, and have to fight to hold on to what you have, however the change comes in loosening your grip on the belief that progress is scarce and competitive. In the words of motivational speaker Zig Ziglar, "You can have everything in life you want, if you will just help other people get what they want." This philosophy underscores that success is not a limited resource—it multiplies when shared.

## How to Install New Beliefs

To install new, empowering beliefs, follow these steps:

1. **Identify Limiting Beliefs:** Start by recognizing the beliefs that hold you back. These might be thoughts like "I'm not good enough" or "I'll never succeed." Journaling your thoughts can help you become more aware of these patterns.

2. **Challenge Old Beliefs:** Once you've identified limiting beliefs, challenge them with evidence to the contrary. Ask yourself if these beliefs are based on reality or past experiences that no longer apply.

3. **Create New Affirmations:** Develop positive affirmations to replace old beliefs. For example, if you believe "I'm not good enough," replace it with "I am capable and deserving of success."

4. **Repeat and Reinforce:** Repeat your new affirmations daily, especially during times of stress or uncertainty. Consistency is key to making these beliefs stick.

5. **Visualize Success:** Use visualization techniques to imagine yourself achieving your goals. This helps your brain believe that success is possible, making it more likely to happen.

By installing new, empowering beliefs, you begin to shift your mindset towards success. Remember, this process takes time and consistency, but the results can be transformative.

## 2.4 Hacking Your Brain Chemistry for Motivation & Focus

Imagine having the power to supercharge your motivation and clarity by tapping directly into the chemistry of your brain. In this section, we explore the intricate dance of neurotransmitters—especially dopamine—and how understanding this process can empower you to intentionally boost your mental energy. We'll reveal the science behind why feeling good is not just a luxury but a cornerstone of success, and offer daily practices that recalibrate your brain for peak performance.

### How Dopamine Affects Your Motivation—and How to Hack It

Dopamine is often celebrated as the "feel-good" chemical, yet its role extends far beyond merely making you smile. It is the engine that propels you toward your goals, fueling the drive to pursue rewards both big and small. When you set a goal—whether it's completing a morning jog or launching a groundbreaking business—dopamine surges, nudging you forward with a burst of energy and determination. After years of rejection, a newly reentering citizen can set daily micro-goals (filling out one application, refining one skill). Each success is a dopamine hit building unstoppable momentum.

## The Motivation Molecule

Neuroscientists have long recognized dopamine as a key player in motivation. But what's truly fascinating is that dopamine doesn't simply respond to success—it anticipates it. Every time you vividly visualize achieving an objective, your brain releases a small burst of dopamine, reinforcing your drive and creating a tangible sense of excitement for what's to come. As Dr. Andrew Huberman explains, this anticipatory dopamine release is critical for sustaining motivation, effectively "tricking" your brain into staying engaged even when the journey is long and arduous.

Before an athlete steps onto the field, that surge of expectation isn't just adrenaline—it's a carefully orchestrated release of dopamine preparing the body and mind for peak performance. This mechanism means that your brain is actively training for success every time you dare to dream vividly.

Motivation and focus are crucial for achieving success, but they can be elusive when you're struggling to break free from old patterns and rebuild your life. Fortunately, there are practical techniques to hack your brain chemistry and boost your motivation and focus.

## Practical Techniques for Boosting Motivation and Focus

1. **Dopamine Boosters:** Dopamine is the neurotransmitter associated with pleasure and reward. To boost dopamine levels, engage in activities that bring you joy, such as hobbies or spending time with loved ones. Celebrate small victories to reinforce positive behaviors.

2. **Exercise and Physical Activity:** Exercise is a powerful way to increase dopamine and improve focus. Regular physical activity can help you stay motivated by releasing endorphins, which enhance mood and energy levels.

3. **Mindfulness and Meditation:** Mindfulness practices help improve focus by training your brain to stay present. Regular meditation can also reduce stress and increase motivation by enhancing self-awareness.

4. **Nutrition and Sleep:** A balanced diet rich in omega-3 fatty acids and vitamins can support brain health, improving focus and motivation. Adequate sleep is also crucial, as it helps consolidate memories and regulate emotions.

5. **Goal Setting:** Set clear, achievable goals to maintain motivation. Break down large goals into smaller, manageable steps to avoid feeling overwhelmed.

# Chapter 2 Case Study: Shaka Senghor

## Background:

Shaka Senghor was raised in a middle-class neighborhood on Detroit's east side during the 1980s. Despite being an honor roll student with aspirations of becoming a doctor, his life took a drastic turn at age 11 when his parents' marriage began to unravel, leading to abuse and instability at home. At 14, he ran away and became involved in the drug trade. In 1991, at the age of 19, Senghor shot and killed a man named David Vaughn during a drug-related confrontation, leading to a conviction for second-degree murder in Michigan. He served 19 years in prison, including seven years in solitary confinement.

## Application of Principles:

- **Understanding Neuroplasticity:** While incarcerated, Senghor discovered literature and began to educate himself, realizing that he could rewire his brain by forming new, positive neural connections through continuous learning and self-reflection.

- **Identity-Based Habits:** He adopted the identity of a writer and intellectual, consistently engaging in reading and writing, which reinforced his transformation and distanced him from his past behaviors.

- **Mental Rehearsal:** Senghor utilized visualization techniques to mentally rehearse his future as a positive contributor to society, preparing himself for a successful reintegration post-incarceration.

## Outcome:

Upon his release in 2010, Senghor became a prominent author, speaker, and advocate for criminal justice reform. His memoir, *Writing My Wrongs: Life, Death, and Redemption in an American Prison*, became a New York Times bestseller, offering profound insights into his journey of transformation. He has lectured at universities, including the University of Michigan and the MIT Media Lab, sharing his experiences to inspire others and promote systemic change.

## 2.5 Action Plan - Rewire Your Thought Patterns for Success

Now that you've learned about the power of thought and how to break free from old habits, it's time to put these concepts into action. The following plan is designed to help you rewire your thought patterns and align them with your goals for success.

**Weekly Thought Transformation Plan**

1. **Identify Negative Thought Patterns (10 minutes):**

   - Start each week by journaling your thoughts and emotions. Identify any negative patterns or self-doubt that arise.

   - Reflect on how these thoughts have held you back in the past.

2. **Challenge Negative Beliefs (15 minutes):**

   - Once you've identified negative thought patterns, challenge them with evidence to the contrary. Ask yourself if these beliefs are based on reality or past experiences that no longer apply.

   - Write down three reasons why these beliefs are not true.

3. **Create Positive Affirmations (10 minutes):**

   - Develop positive affirmations to replace old beliefs. For example, if you believe "I'm not good enough," replace it with "I am capable and deserving of success."

- Repeat these affirmations daily, especially during times of stress or uncertainty.

4. **Practice Mindfulness (20 minutes):**

    - Engage in mindfulness exercises to become more aware of your thoughts and emotions. This can be meditation, deep breathing, or simply focusing on the present moment.

    - Use this time to let go of past regrets or future anxieties.

5. **Visualize Success (15 minutes):**

    - Use visualization techniques to imagine yourself achieving your goals. Picture yourself succeeding and overcoming challenges.

    - Reflect on how achieving these goals will make you feel and what steps you need to take to get there.

## Monthly Reflection and Adjustment

- **Assess Your Progress:** Take time to reflect on how far you've come. Identify areas where you've improved and where you still need to work.

- **Adjust Your Plan:** Based on your reflections, adjust your weekly practices to better align with your goals.

### Additional Strategies for Success

1. **Build a Support Network:** Surround yourself with people who support and believe in your potential. This could include friends, family, or a mentor.

2. **Set Realistic Goals:** Define what you want to achieve and create a plan to get there. Break down large goals into smaller, manageable steps to avoid feeling overwhelmed.

3. **Practice Self-Care:** Engage in activities that nourish your mind, body, and soul. This could be exercise, reading, or spending time in nature.

4. **Learn to Forgive Yourself:** Recognize that past mistakes are not

defining characteristics. Practice self-forgiveness and focus on moving forward.

5. **Celebrate Small Wins:** Acknowledge and celebrate each small victory along the way. This helps build confidence and reinforces positive behaviors.

By following this action plan, you'll begin to rewire your thought patterns, aligning them with your goals for success. Remember, transformation is a journey, and every small step counts.

## Chapter 2 Summary: Rewiring Your Brain for Success – Harnessing the Science of Transformation

You now understand that your thoughts are more than fleeting ideas—they are the architects of your reality. Every time you challenge a limiting belief, reframe a negative thought, or practice intentional mental reprogramming, you are literally reshaping your brain for success.

In this chapter, you discovered that no matter what you've been through—whether it's incarceration, financial struggles, or deep personal trauma—your brain retains an incredible ability to adapt, evolve, and grow. You've learned that breaking free from the past starts with breaking free from your old self—letting go of outdated habits, rewiring the subconscious patterns that no longer serve you, and replacing them with intentional thoughts, beliefs, and actions that drive success.

But change isn't just about mindset—it's about chemistry, too. By understanding how dopamine and neuroplasticity fuel motivation and learning, you now have the power to optimize your brain for growth. The success mindset formula gave you the blueprint for sustained transformation, showing you how to align your beliefs, habits, and actions to create a reality that works in your favor.

Now, it's time to face the biggest roadblock to lasting change—fear.

In Chapter 3, we'll confront the mental and emotional traps that keep you stuck—fear of failure, fear of success, and the self-doubt that tries to convince you that you're not capable of more. You'll learn how to break free from these invisible chains so that nothing—not past mistakes, not negative self-talk, not the fear of judgment—can hold you back from stepping into the life you deserve.

# Chapter 3

# Overcoming Fear and Self-Doubt – Breaking the Chains Holding You Back

*"Fear kills more dreams than failure ever will."* – Suzy Kassem

Fear is the invisible force that often keeps us stuck in mediocrity. It lurks in the shadows, whispering doubts and convincing us that risk is too dangerous, that change is too overwhelming, especially when the world has labeled us unfit—perhaps due to a criminal record, devastating loss, or deep personal crisis. Yet, when we examine fear for what it truly is—a series of mental illusions—its power begins to wane. In this chapter, you'll find the courage and tools to overcome fear, dismantle self-doubt, and move beyond victimhood, empowering you to embrace the life you truly deserve.

## Preview – Meet Monica Lewinsky

Have you ever felt paralyzed by fear, self-doubt, or shame? Monica Lewinsky has. In her early twenties, Monica became the center of a humiliating public scandal. Victimized and exploited, she could have remained hidden, forever trapped by shame and fear of judgment. Instead, Monica chose courage. Her story reveals how anyone can overcome the fear of failure—and even the fear of success—to reclaim personal power and dignity.

Monica's inspiring story continues at the end of this chapter, revealing the steps she took to overcome fear and reclaim her power.

# 3.1 Understanding the Root of Fear

To overcome fear, we must first understand its origins. By delving into the biological and psychological underpinnings of fear, we can begin to dismantle the barriers it creates.

## The Biology of Fear – Why Your Brain Is Wired for Survival, Not Success

Our brains are marvels of evolution, designed primarily for survival. At the core of this design lies a powerful system known as the amygdala—a small, almond-shaped structure that triggers a fight-or-flight response at the slightest hint of danger. This response, while crucial in a prehistoric world full of predators, can become maladaptive in our modern lives. The brain, in its default mode, is wired to protect us, sometimes at the expense of our growth and success.

For example, picture how your body reacts to the anticipation of public speaking or the prospect of failure. The surge of adrenaline, the rapid heartbeat, and even the trembling hands are all signs that your brain is preparing for a threat. Neuroscientists like Joseph LeDoux have demonstrated that this primal wiring, although life-saving in its original context, often hampers our ability to pursue new opportunities. Instead of empowering us, these biological impulses create a loop of anxiety that stifles creativity and risk-taking.

## How Fear Keeps You Stuck – The Subconscious Mind Clings to the Familiar

Fear often thrives on familiarity, a comfort found in predictability, even when that predictability means enduring repeated disappointments. The subconscious mind, a repository of every experience we have ever had, clings to the known, even if it is painful. This is why fear can become a self-perpetuating cycle.

In my own journey, I experienced this firsthand. For several years after my arrest, during my probation, I lived with the constant fear that if someone Googled my name, all my hard work to establish a business would come crashing down and I would face public shame and humiliation all over again. I'd work up the courage to ask for permission to expand my business into neighboring counties by going to court, but despite receiving green lights from judges and probation, I chose to remain small when it came down to putting myself out there. Everything constantly felt like it could be taken away in a moment. My conscious desire to succeed was overshadowed by my subconscious, which held tightly to past experiences. This pattern of self-sabotage kept me locked in mediocrity, reinforcing the fear that had become so familiar.

This cycle of fear and self-sabotage is not unique to my experience. Many people find themselves trapped in similar patterns, where the comfort of familiarity outweighs the risk of change. However, recognizing this pattern is the first step towards breaking free. By acknowledging how fear can hold us back, we can begin to challenge these beliefs and create a new narrative for our lives.

This clinging to the familiar is not a failure of willpower but a natural, albeit counterproductive, defense mechanism. However, when fear dominates, our subconscious plays it safe, stifling the very vulnerability that could lead us to breakthroughs. The challenge lies in retraining our minds to embrace uncertainty and view the unfamiliar not as a threat, but as a canvas for growth.

## Separating Real vs. Imaginary Fear – How to Identify What's Truly Dangerous vs. What's Holding You Back

Not all fear is created equal. Some fears are rational—protecting us from genuine harm—while others are imaginary constructs that serve only to limit our potential. Learning to distinguish between the two is a critical step in overcoming self-doubt. Ask yourself: What am I truly afraid of? Is it the possibility of physical harm, or is it the fear of being judged, of not living up to expectations?

For years I spent so much time agonizing over whether I should attempt to re-establish myself publicly and professionally, my mind a swirling mix of "what ifs" and worst-case scenarios. Eventually, I began to dissect these fears, questioning which ones had a basis in reality and which were mere projections of my insecurities. I discovered that the fear of being identified was less about the act itself and more about the potential for judgment and re-traumatization from local news media—a fear that, while understandable, was largely imagined. By separating real danger from imagined threats, I was able to focus on preparation and skill-building, rather than being paralyzed by what-ifs.

This process of discernment is supported by cognitive behavioral strategies that encourage you to confront your fears head-on. As Dr. David Burns explains, "When you challenge your thoughts, you challenge your feelings." By systematically evaluating your fears, you can begin to weaken the grip of those that are baseless, paving the way for a more rational, empowered mindset.

## 3.2  Overcoming the Fear of Failure

Failure is often painted as the end of the road—a final, crushing verdict on our worth and ability. Yet, in the realm of success, failure is not the enemy but an essential teacher. Let's delve into the transformative power of failure, exploring why it is crucial for growth, how to reframe it as valuable feedback, and practical ways to take risks without succumbing to fear.

### Why Failure Is Essential for Success

Failure is a natural part of any meaningful journey. It's not a sign of weakness; rather, it is the crucible in which resilience and ingenuity are forged. Think of failure as a trial by fire—a necessary process that burns away the inessential and leaves behind only the most refined version of our potential.

Scientific research in psychology supports this idea. Studies show that experiencing setbacks can actually enhance problem-solving skills and boost creativity. When you encounter failure, your brain is forced to adapt, to search for alternative strategies, and in the process, you develop a deeper understanding of what works. Without my failures, I might never have discovered a more effective strategy for navigating life—a strategy that eventually led to success.

Imagine the moment someone attempts to start a small business after reentry—overcoming denials, rejections, or endless questions about their past. Each "no" can be a springboard rather than a dead end, revealing the angles or details that need refining. Without those so-called failures, the strategy that ultimately leads to success might remain undiscovered. Mistakes are not permanent verdicts on our ability. Failure, therefore, should be embraced as an integral part of the learning process. It strips away the fear of imperfection and opens the door to experimentation, innovation, and growth.

## Reframing Failure as Feedback

The key to overcoming the fear of failure lies in reframing it as feedback rather than a final judgment on your abilities. Instead of perceiving a setback as evidence of your limitations, view it as a constructive response from the universe—a signal that guides you toward improvement. When you reframe failure in this way, every mistake becomes a data point, offering insights into what might be tweaked, refined, or completely reimagined. This shift in perspective transforms every failure into a stepping stone, a necessary detour on the road to mastery. In this way, failure ceases to be a mark of defeat and becomes a vital component of the feedback loop that propels you toward success.

## Actionable Ways to Take Risks Without Fear

Taking risks is often the most daunting part of any venture, especially when the specter of failure looms large. Yet, risk-taking is essential for growth. The key is to approach risks methodically—by breaking them down into manageable parts and preparing yourself to learn from every outcome.

One effective strategy is to set small, incremental challenges for yourself. For instance, if the idea of public speaking terrifies you, start by speaking up in a small meeting or joining a local discussion group. These low-stakes opportunities allow you to build confidence gradually. With each small risk you take, the intensity of fear diminishes, and is replaced by a growing sense of empowerment. Over time, these minor victories accumulate, enabling you to tackle larger challenges with a newfound courage.

Another actionable approach is to conduct a "risk analysis" before you act. Write down your fears and the worst-case scenario, and then realistically assess the likelihood and impact of that outcome. Often, you'll find that the potential negative consequences are far less catastrophic than your mind imagines. This rational approach, endorsed by experts in decision-making and behavioral psychology, helps to demystify fear and makes the act of taking risks feel more like a calculated step rather than a leap into the unknown.

Additionally, surround yourself with a support network that encourages you to push beyond your comfort zone. Engage with mentors, peers, or even supportive online communities that celebrate experimentation and growth. Their encouragement can provide both the accountability and the reassurance needed to take risks. Remember the words of Dr. Brené Brown: "Vulnerability is the birthplace of innovation, creativity, and change." Embracing vulnerability—by taking risks despite the fear of failure—is how you unlock your true potential.

These principles hold true whether you're grappling with deeply rooted poverty, social stigma, or the emotional aftermath of trauma. The ultimate takeaway is hopeful: real, lasting success often thrives in the spaces where fear dared you not to tread. By seeing failure as a teacher and risk as an invitation, you tap into your inherent capacity to reshape both your mindset and your future.

## 3.3 Destroying the Fear of Success

*"Success is not final; failure is not fatal: it is the courage to continue that counts."* – Winston Churchill

The notion that success itself could be more terrifying than failure seems counterintuitive at first. Failure carries disappointment, regret, and pain; success is supposed to be the desired outcome—right? Yet, many people discover that the fear of their own potential can be more paralyzing than any misstep they've experienced. Let's examine the psychological roots behind that anxiety, explore how subconscious forces might sabotage our upward momentum, and outline practical steps to embrace success fully—even in the face of traumatic histories, public stigma, or the harsh scrutiny that comes with shedding old labels.

## Why Success Scares People More Than Failure

At its core, success triggers deep-seated anxieties about change, visibility, and the weight of new responsibilities. Social psychology research suggests that individuals who rise above their entrenched circumstances—like those who have been marginalized due to incarceration, generational poverty, or systemic discrimination—often fear that success will shine a spotlight on parts of themselves they're not ready to share. It's the sense that stepping into a better life also opens you up to heightened expectations and potential judgment.

Several years ago, I was offered a chance to teach alongside my mentor—a dream opportunity that should have filled me with excitement. Instead, I felt a wave of panic. What if I wasn't capable? What if I let her down? What if I failed in front of everyone? But there was another fear lurking beneath the surface: the fear of succeeding. What if I succeeded and was suddenly expected to keep succeeding, to carry on her legacy?

Growing up, I had strong female mentors who were trailblazers in their fields. My mother was particularly successful, and I often felt the weight of living up to her successes. Despite being a good student and developing valuable skills under their guidance, I subconsciously believed that success meant meeting an impossible standard. The pedestal I placed these women on was too high, and the thought of being seen as someone on their level made me retreat into self-doubt.

This fear of success led me to sabotage my own potential. I would stop short of achieving my goals, fearing the pressure of being held to a higher standard. This pattern of self-doubt and fear ultimately led to a series of devastating consequences, including a public scandal and criminal charges. I lost my reputation, dignity, and freedom, spending years in hiding to recover and rebuild.

Looking back, I realize that my fear of success was not just about failing; it was about not being worthy of success. It was a deeply ingrained belief that I wasn't good enough, that I didn't belong, and that I was unworthy of love. This fear was a silent influencer, guiding my actions and decisions without me even realizing it.

To break free from this fear, I had to confront it head-on. I began by acknowledging the negative beliefs that held me back and challenging them with new, positive affirmations. I practiced self-forgiveness and learned to see my past mistakes as opportunities for growth rather than defining characteristics.

## Success Exposes Vulnerabilities

When you succeed, you're no longer able to hide behind the comforts of routine disappointment. The moment you break through old limitations, a new reality emerges—often with less room to explain away shortcomings as "the norm." This process can unearth emotions or insecurities that have long been swept aside. According to Dr. Abraham Maslow's studies on human potential, achieving upward steps in life's hierarchy often demands facing unresolved layers of fear.

Moreover, success requires continual adaptation. If someone transitions from being unhoused to stable housing, or from unemployment to a managerial role, each step forward forces a redefinition of identity. That redefinition can feel unnerving, as if the stable ground of old struggles is replaced by the uneasy possibility of "What if I can't maintain this?" or "What if I can't meet these new expectations?" When fear whispers that success is fragile, the mind often reverts to self-limiting patterns for emotional safety.

## Society's Shifting Expectations

For those coming out of significant trauma—an abusive upbringing, a series of devastating losses, or time served in the criminal justice system—success can also provoke external pressures. Friends, family, or even the public might cheer you on initially, yet they might also scrutinize your every move under the assumption that your success is an anomaly. Such scrutiny can be suffocating, reinforcing the idea that it may be easier to stay "comfortably stuck" than to bear the weight of being a role model or a token example of reform.

## How Your Subconscious Might Be Sabotaging Your Success

The subconscious is like a hidden director, orchestrating life from behind the scenes. Early experiences of dismissal—like hearing "You'll never be anything" or "People like you can't succeed"—can program the mind to resist progress. Even when your conscious mind yearns for a brighter outcome, your subconscious may cling to past narratives or the "safety net" of familiar disappointments.

## Internal Narratives That Undermine Progress

A talented individual might repeatedly underperform during critical moments. Despite outward capability, their subconscious replays messages of unworthiness, preventing them from truly committing to victory. The moment success appears on the horizon, old beliefs like "You don't deserve this" or "Everyone will find out you're a fraud" can surface, causing hesitation or self-sabotage.

I have always been considered the girl with "so much potential" and yet often quit jobs, changed trajectories completely, or in the case of my arrest, completely sabotaged my whole life. What should have been a survival instinct to protect myself from devastating outcomes was instead an opportunity for my *fear of success* programming to keep me falling short from living up to my potential.

Behavioral psychology points out that brains wired for survival will sometimes treat success as a "threat." Stepping into a better life can disrupt the comfort zone—like when a reentering citizen is offered a promotion but feels haunted by the question "Do I really fit here?" That lingering doubt, fueled by past rejections and labels, can trigger subtle acts of sabotage: missing deadlines, avoiding necessary confrontations, or refusing mentorship. According to Dr. Dan Siegel, our internal narratives are deeply influenced by past experiences. For those who have faced rejection or systemic barriers, the idea of success can trigger feelings of discomfort or self-doubt. By becoming aware of these narratives through mindfulness, individuals can begin to rewire their responses to new opportunities, embracing vulnerability as a path to growth rather than a threat to their sense of self.

## Rewriting Subconscious Scripts

Identifying the core fear behind sabotaging behavior is half the battle. Some people discover it's not failure they fear, but the potential cost of stepping into a bigger life: alienating old friends, confronting deeper insecurities, or outgrowing family expectations. Once these hidden saboteurs are brought to light, the task becomes rewriting the script. This involves a two-part process:

1. **Reflection:** Pinpoint which subconscious messages are repeated from past grievances, social stigma, or family conditioning.

2. **Reprogramming:** Replace those messages with concrete affirmations of your capability and worth, grounding them in daily actions that prove your readiness for growth.

By methodically challenging the voice that says "Stay small," you affirm a new identity: one that sees success not as an intrusion, but as a natural extension of your potential. Psychologists assert that awareness of the subconscious mind is what transforms it from an invisible puppeteer into a supportive collaborator.

## Building a Foundation of Trust in Your Own Potential

Overcoming the fear of success means relearning trust—trust in your skills, your instincts, and your ability to adapt even when the stakes are high. People who emerge from systemic barriers know all too well that society isn't always prepared to celebrate their breakthroughs; in fact, institutions may even place extra burdens on their newfound achievements. Yet, as you break free from self-doubt, you also dismantle the internal ceilings that once held you back.

- **Acknowledge** that success will change your life—and that change can be positive.

- **Pinpoint** the subconscious blocks that trigger sabotage.

- **Consciously** replace old beliefs with affirmations and habits that match your evolving self.

When you gradually reframe success as an exciting frontier rather than a threat, you take control of the narrative. Each small step away from the known and into the realm of possibility asserts your right to thrive. The fear of success no longer keeps you bound in mediocrity but becomes a challenge—one you are equipped to meet, thanks to the resilience you've forged through hardships and the clarity you've gained from reflection.

### Practical Steps to Embrace and Welcome Success

### 1. Acknowledge Your Fears

Fear thrives in hidden corners. Draw it into the light by naming each anxiety that surfaces at the thought of achieving something bigger—whether it's the fear of living up to new responsibilities, being judged by society, or confronting personal shortcomings you've tried to ignore. Write these worries down in a journal. Psychologist Susan David reminds us that *"Feelings are data."* By articulating them, you start transforming fear from a looming presence into a concrete set of challenges you can tackle.

Think about someone facing the stigma of a criminal record who finally sees a door open—a managerial position or a chance at entrepreneurship. The moment success beckons, anxieties about public scrutiny or being labeled a "token hire" can arise. Naming these fears reduces the power they hold, turning them into tangible issues with specific solutions (such as seeking mentorship or clarifying expectations up front).

## 2. Reframe Success as Growth

Substitute "If I succeed, everything will change" with "Success is a step in my ongoing evolution." This adjustment reflects what Dr. Carol Dweck calls a "growth mindset," reframing success from a dramatic endpoint into a dynamic phase of personal development. Each success story—especially among those who have fought uphill battles against socio-economic barriers or the label of a felony conviction—serves as evidence that evolution is continual, not a one-time event.

By shifting your focus to *progress over perfection*, you reduce the pressure that makes success feel overwhelming. If you're transitioning from survival mode (uncertain housing, limited opportunities) to a more stable life, celebrate each incremental advancement instead of fearing the day you have "made it."

## 3. Set Incremental Goals

Big achievements can evoke fears of being unable to handle the spotlight or the demands that follow. Tackle these concerns by breaking major goals into smaller, manageable tasks. Celebrate even minor milestones—like speaking up in a small meeting if you're terrified of public recognition, or posting a creative project in a supportive online forum if you're anxious about judgment.

Positive reinforcement plays a crucial role here. Your brain learns to associate success with affirming emotions rather than dread. Each low-stakes victory paves the way for more visible, higher-stakes successes down the line. This approach is invaluable for those climbing out of long-term adversity—every small step builds momentum, reinforcing a sense of capability and validating your potential for greater heights.

## 4. Cultivate a Supportive Network

Surround yourself with individuals who celebrate your wins and champion your progress. Whether it's a professional group, an advocacy community, or a mentor who has navigated similar hardships, a supportive network elevates your perspective. When you collaborate with people who share aspirations for growth—especially those familiar with systemic injustice or past trauma—you're more likely to maintain the courage it takes to keep moving forward.

If you've felt alone in your journey—maybe because stigma has pushed you to hide parts of your history—connecting with likeminded folks reminds you that you're not isolated in your ambition. It can be an online group for entrepreneurs with lived experience or a grassroots initiative supporting returning citizens. Strength in numbers reduces the fear that success will leave you alienated or misunderstood.

## 5. Practice Self-Compassion

Success isn't about flawlessness. It's about risk-taking and learning at every turn. When missteps happen, respond with the same kindness you'd offer a friend in crisis. Self-compassion neutralizes the harsh inner critic that so often derails promising progress. Dr. Kristin Neff, a pioneer in this field, points out that *"Self-compassion is a powerful antidote to perfectionism and self-doubt."*

This principle is crucial for those who have experienced repeated societal dismissal—like failing a background check for the tenth time or facing skepticism in a family that doubts your ability to stay on the right path. Instead of berating yourself—"I knew I wouldn't measure up"—treat each stumbling block as a lesson, a necessary piece of growth. A compassionate stance allows you to navigate setbacks without spiraling back into old narratives.

## Putting It All Together: A Life Open to Success

Embracing success requires a deliberate shift in how you perceive risk, achievement, and personal evolution. Each of these strategies—acknowledging fears, reframing success, incremental goals, cultivating support, and self-compassion—forms a collective blueprint for transcending the limits fear imposes. Whether you're wrestling with the complexities of reentry, the weight of a traumatic past, or simply the daunting idea of living beyond the status quo, these steps offer a scaffold for turning apprehension into opportunity. By taking them one at a time, you'll find that success ceases to be a threat and transforms into a bold new chapter of your ongoing journey.

### Real-World Resilience: Amy Purdy's Courageous Comeback

At just 19 years old, Amy Purdy's life was changed forever when she contracted bacterial meningitis. She lost both of her legs below the knee, her spleen, and her kidneys. Doctors told Amy that walking again would be nearly impossible, let alone pursuing her passions like snowboarding and dancing. Filled with fear and self-doubt, Amy struggled with the overwhelming uncertainty of what her life could become.

But Amy decided her story wouldn't be defined by fear. Refusing to accept her physical limitations as permanent, she courageously confronted her deepest doubts and fears. With perseverance, Amy returned to snowboarding, eventually becoming a Paralympic medalist and a finalist on "Dancing with the Stars." Today, Amy inspires millions as a motivational speaker and author, teaching others to break through fear, redefine limitations, and achieve what once seemed impossible.

Amy's journey teaches us that fear and self-doubt lose their power when we decide to face them head-on. Her extraordinary life shows what's possible when we choose courage over comfort.

## 3.4  Eliminating Self-Doubt Once and for All

Self-doubt operates like a low-lying fog—easy to dismiss at first, yet it obscures every next step unless deliberately cleared. It whispers that you're unworthy, that your past mistakes outweigh your potential, or that social barriers will never allow you to rise. Whether that whisper comes from years of stigma tied to a criminal history, the trauma of repeated job rejections, or the raw aftermath of personal loss, self-doubt can become an ever-present adversary.

# How to Stop Comparing Yourself to Others

*"To be yourself in a world that is constantly trying to make you something else is the greatest accomplishment."*– Ralph Waldo Emerson

Comparison robs us of progress by focusing our attention on external markers instead of our own consistent growth. In an age dominated by social media, it's tempting to measure your self-worth against the curated highlights of others—perhaps the neighbor who swiftly overcame their record and started a thriving business, or the influencer whose feed radiates effortless success. Such comparisons can feel especially suffocating if you're fighting an uphill battle—like pushing through financial instability, or working to reestablish your reputation post-incarceration.

## The Toxic Cycle of Comparison

Scrolling through endless images of other people's achievements can trigger thoughts of "Why not me?" or "I'm so far behind." This cycle hinders your ability to see your own path as valid, especially if your journey includes legal constraints, systemic discrimination, or unresolved trauma. Psychologists warn that constant comparison is a breeding ground for self-doubt and perceived inadequacy.

A turning point emerges when you shift your focus from external benchmarks to internal milestones. Some find value in documenting small victories—like completing an application despite the fear of rejection, or following through on a self-care routine that fosters emotional well-being. Over time, these personal logs highlight how much you're actually accomplishing, even if it doesn't fit someone else's timeline or standard.

## Reducing the Comparison Triggers

- **Curb Social Media Exposure:** Unfollow accounts that feed a sense of inadequacy; follow those that share real, nuanced stories of growth or that celebrate resilience rather than perfection.

- **Re-evaluate Your Online Feeds:** Many advocates suggest a "digital detox" for those grappling with the mental toll of reentry or intense personal challenges. Freed from a barrage of highlight reels, it's easier to see your life as a valid work in progress.

- **Build a Supportive Network:** Engage with communities—online or in person—that prioritize authenticity and collective empowerment. Whether it's a reentry group focusing on skill-building or a mutual support collective for trauma survivors, these spaces shift attention from "What do I lack?" to "How can we grow together?"

## Owning Your Distinct Timeline

No two lives unfold identically. Someone may secure stable employment right after leaving a correctional facility, while another may require months (or years) of incremental steps—GED classes, substance recovery programs, or creative business endeavors. The essential truth remains: your journey is your own. Each stride forward, each obstacle overcome, reflects a personal tapestry of effort, resilience, and ambition.

When comparison is no longer an automatic reflex, creativity flourishes—not just artistic or entrepreneurial creativity, but also the creativity to devise solutions that honor your experiences. Distancing yourself from constant external measurements grants space to refine the vision of what you can become, free of the self-doubt that comparison so often stirs.

## Building Unshakable Self-Trust

Eliminating self-doubt hinges on cultivating self-trust—the deep-seated belief that your instincts, decisions, and history of overcoming obstacles will guide you through life's complexities. This trust acts as a cornerstone for genuine confidence, offering the quiet conviction that no matter what challenges surface—be it social stigma, legal constraints, or the emotional weight of past harm—you possess the internal resources to adapt and thrive.

## Honoring Your Experiences

Developing self-trust begins with acknowledging the value of your personal journey. If you've navigated the court system, survived a major loss, or borne the label of "offender" or "victim," each step has tested your resilience. Reflecting on those moments—especially the tough choices that led to growth—provides tangible proof that you can endure adversity.

Experts such as Tony Robbins stress that true leadership begins with self-belief. Trusting your own capacity for growth creates a positive feedback loop, reinforcing your sense of self-worth and deterring the habit of second-guessing each move. Self-trust also involves accepting that missteps are inherent in learning. Rather than a verdict of inadequacy, each failure can become a lesson—a stepping stone toward refinement.

## The Ongoing Journey of Self-Trust

Constructing unshakable self-trust rarely happens overnight. It's a gradual process where every act of trusting yourself—whether it's applying for a job despite a criminal record, advocating for your needs in a legal hearing, or speaking up in a setting that once felt hostile—strengthens an inner voice committed to your well-being. Each small victory expands the possibility for larger transformations, transforming self-doubt from a daily burden into a distant echo.

In communities shaped by gatekeeping tactics—where your prior mistakes or vulnerabilities can be weaponized against you—cultivating self-trust proves especially crucial. The deliberate choice to rely on one's own insight fosters the resilience needed to press on, even when external validation remains scarce. With every step taken in confidence, the barriers that once seemed insurmountable gradually lose their power, clearing a path toward a life guided by purpose and conviction.

# Chapter 3 Case Study: Monica Lewinsky

## Background:

In 1998, Monica Lewinsky found herself at the center of one of the most widely publicized scandals in modern American history. At the age of 22, Lewinsky, then a White House intern, was thrust into the global spotlight due to her intimate relationship with President Bill Clinton. The exposure of this relationship resulted in relentless public humiliation, exploitation by the media, and lasting trauma that deeply affected her self-esteem and personal identity.

Initially, Lewinsky retreated from public life, crippled by fear of further judgment and self-doubt stemming from years of intense scrutiny and shaming.

## Application of Principles:

- **Confronting Fear of Judgment and Failure:**

  Lewinsky recognized that the shame and fear that kept her hidden were emotional traps that prevented her from moving forward. By openly acknowledging her experiences in her TED Talk, "The Price of Shame," she directly faced her fears, transforming vulnerability into strength and public support.

- **Transforming the Victim Mindset:**

  Rather than remaining trapped in victimhood, Lewinsky consciously reframed her narrative. She chose to publicly acknowledge her trauma and vulnerability, transforming feelings of shame into a powerful tool for social advocacy and compassion.

- **Radical Self-Compassion:**

  Lewinsky deliberately chose self-compassion over self-blame, openly speaking about her journey toward forgiving herself. This practice allowed her to rebuild her confidence, dismantling the emotional traps of fear and shame that previously kept her isolated.

- **Advocacy and Social Impact:**

    Lewinsky used her painful experiences as the foundation for advocacy, directly challenging the societal narratives that perpetuated exploitation and public humiliation.

## Outcome:

Today, Monica Lewinsky is an internationally recognized speaker, writer, and advocate against cyberbullying and public shaming. Her powerful TED Talk, "The Price of Shame," has been viewed millions of times, inspiring countless others to reclaim their narratives, move beyond victimhood, and embrace their power to heal and create positive societal change. Through her bravery in confronting personal fears and openly discussing her experiences, Lewinsky has successfully turned past exploitation into empowerment—not just for herself, but for millions affected by shame and public humiliation.

## 3.5 Action Plan - Face and Conquer Fear Daily

Now that you've learned about the root of fear and how to overcome it, it's time to put these concepts into action. The following plan is designed to help you face and conquer fear daily, aligning with your goals for success.

**Daily Fear-Conquering Plan**

1. **Morning Reflection (10 minutes):**
    - Start each day by journaling your thoughts and emotions. Identify any fears or doubts that arise.
    - Reflect on how these fears have held you back in the past.

2. **Fear Reframing (15 minutes):**
    - Once you've identified your fears, reframe them in a positive light. For example, instead of "I fear failure," say "I am capable of learning from my mistakes."
    - Write down three reasons why these fears are not insurmountable.

3. **Visualization Exercise (15 minutes):**

   - Use visualization techniques to imagine yourself overcoming your fears. Picture yourself succeeding and overcoming challenges.

   - Reflect on how achieving these goals will make you feel and what steps you need to take to get there.

4. **Daily Action Towards Goals (30 minutes):**

   - Take small, consistent actions towards your goals each day. This helps build confidence and reinforces positive behaviors.

   - Celebrate each small victory along the way.

5. **Evening Review (10 minutes):**

   - Before bed, review your day. Identify moments where you successfully faced your fears or overcame self-doubt.

   - Plan how you can build on these successes tomorrow.

## Weekly Challenge

- **Identify and Confront One Major Fear:** Choose one significant fear that holds you back and confront it each week. Develop a plan to address this fear and take consistent action towards overcoming it.

- **Share Your Progress:** Share your progress with a trusted friend or mentor. This can help keep you accountable and motivated.

## Monthly Reflection and Adjustment

- **Assess Your Progress:** Take time to reflect on how far you've come. Identify areas where you've improved and where you still need to work.

- **Adjust Your Plan:** Based on your reflections, adjust your daily and weekly practices to better align with your goals.

## Additional Strategies for Success

1. **Build a Support Network:** Surround yourself with people who support and believe in your potential. This could include friends, family, or a mentor.

2. **Practice Mindfulness:** Engage in mindfulness exercises to become more aware of your thoughts and emotions. This can help you manage fear more effectively.

3. **Focus on Past Successes:** Reflect on past successes to build confidence and resilience. This helps reinforce the belief that you can overcome challenges.

4. **Celebrate Small Wins:** Acknowledge and celebrate each small victory along the way. This helps build confidence and reinforces positive behaviors.

By following this action plan, you'll begin to face and conquer fear daily, aligning your mindset with your goals for success. Remember, transformation is a journey, and every small step counts.

# Chapter 3 Summary: Overcoming Fear and Self-Doubt - A Journey to Unleashing Your True Potential

Fear and self-doubt may have shaped your past, but they no longer have to dictate your future. Overcoming fear isn't about eliminating it—it's about learning to move forward despite it. You've now seen how fear is often an outdated survival response, keeping you trapped in comfort zones that no longer serve you.

In this chapter, you explored how fear of failure and fear of success can both act as invisible chains, keeping you from stepping into your full potential. But now, you have the tools to break those chains: treating failure as a stepping stone instead of a stop sign, recognizing and neutralizing self-sabotaging behaviors, and building the confidence to take risks that propel you forward.

Most importantly, you've learned that fear loses its power the moment you take action. Every time you challenge your doubts, step outside your comfort zone, and reframe setbacks as opportunities, you are rewiring your brain for success.

But fear isn't the only thing that holds people back—your environment plays a powerful role in shaping your mindset and future.

In Chapter 4, we'll take a deep dive into toxic patterns, negative influences, and the environments that may be silently sabotaging your progress. You'll learn how to identify and release the people, habits, and surroundings that drain your energy, so you can build a life that supports your growth instead of limiting it.

# Chapter 4

# Breaking Free from Toxic Patterns and Negative Environments

*"The people you surround yourself with are the people you become."* – Tony Robbins

Toxic people, entrenched negative habits, and unsupportive environments often operate like invisible anchors, holding you back in cycles of stagnation, shame, or self-doubt. This chapter exposes the hidden forces that keep you tethered—whether you're wrestling with social stigma from a criminal conviction or trying to rebuild in the aftermath of a devastating personal crisis—and offers practical strategies to break free. By identifying toxic influences, recognizing subtle signs of energy drain, and learning to distance yourself without guilt, you reclaim the power and emotional space needed for growth and fulfillment.

## Preview – Meet Susan Burton

Can you imagine losing everything, including your child, your freedom, and your hope? Susan Burton experienced a mother's worst nightmare—losing her young son. Plunged into addiction and cycles of incarceration, Susan could have remained trapped by her trauma and grief. Instead, she made a brave choice to break away from toxic influences, creating not only a new life for herself but also safe spaces for thousands of other women to rebuild theirs.

You'll find Susan's complete story at the end of this chapter, including how she broke free from the cycles that kept her stuck.

## 4.1 Identifying Toxic People and Energy Drainers

The first step to freeing yourself from negativity is awareness—seeing clearly the influences that sabotage your well-being. Whether these forces stem from peers who perpetually doubt your potential because of past legal troubles, family members who invalidate your experiences, or social circles that undermine your attempts to transition back into society, recognizing them enables you to reshape your environment and initiate transformation.

## The Types of Toxic People to Watch Out For

Toxic individuals appear in many forms, each undermining your mental and emotional resilience. Common types include:

- **The Perpetual Complainer:** Every situation morphs into a crisis, draining your optimism and offering nothing constructive.

- **The Manipulator:** Uses guilt, flattery, or conditional support to exert control—often most visible when you strive for a fresh start post-incarceration or attempt to break generational patterns.

- **The Competitive Rival:** Seeks self-worth by diminishing others; any sign of your progress threatens their sense of superiority.

- **The Empathy-Depleted Critic:** Offers criticism laced with cynicism rather than actionable guidance—validating their own negativity at your expense.

- **The Chronic Victim:** Dodges accountability, shifting blame onto everyone else, and sapping the collective emotional energy.

When you are deeply invested in your successful rebuilding process and start to maintain a positive attitude, you begin to notice when others around you are overwhelmingly negative. Their constant gloominess and unrelenting pessimism weighs down every conversation, which can leave you exhausted and uncertain about your own path. Recognizing these behaviors shed light on a crucial truth: not all insights or opinions are helpful—some are just projections of the speaker's own inner turmoil.

Dr. Harriet Lerner, a noted figure in social psychology, points out that toxic people frequently *mirror unresolved issues within themselves*. This understanding doesn't excuse their conduct but clarifies why their words or actions can erode your self-esteem and progress. Once you identify the patterns and acknowledge them for what they are, you gain the emotional leverage to minimize their impact and safeguard your potential for continued growth.

## Signs Someone Is Draining Your Energy

Toxic energy can manifest in subtle, sometimes hard-to-spot ways. Classic indicators include feeling a wave of exhaustion or hopelessness after interacting with certain people, a nagging sense of unease that lingers for hours, or a noticeable dip in your motivation or creativity. Physical signs—like unexplained headaches or muscle tension—often emerge as the body's somatic response to persistent stress, an issue especially relevant for those trying to rebuild their lives after system involvement, grief, or repeated social rejection.

Recent data from occupational health studies show that chronic exposure to negative interactions—be it in the workplace, community meetings, or social circles—can significantly influence mental well-being and even physical health outcomes. Leading behavioral experts such as Dr. Brené Brown underscore the importance of "constructive connection" for emotional resilience. In other words, it's essential to cultivate supportive relationships that uplift, rather than deplete, your emotional resources.

Recognizing these subtle warning signs—and acknowledging how they might be exacerbated by a history of incarceration, experiences of harm or victimization, or the struggle to navigate reentry—can be the catalyst for reclaiming your emotional balance. Building a network of allies, practicing mindful self-awareness, and implementing healthy boundaries are key steps toward safeguarding both your mental and physical reserves. By staying vigilant about how you feel after spending time with someone, you can more easily identify who or what needs adjusting in your environment, thus protecting the momentum you've worked so hard to rebuild.

In my journey of recovery post-conviction, I found solace in a support group where shared experiences created a sense of understanding and connection.

Being part of a group that had faced similar challenges helped me navigate the isolating world of stigmatizing labels. Watching others succeed while on probation provided me with valuable guidance and clarity.

However, there's a delicate balance between supporting one another and getting caught in a cycle of negativity. It's easy to find comfort in commiserating with others who have also been traumatized, but this can lead to a draining of energy. As the saying goes, "misery loves company." True support comes from acknowledging shared pain and then redirecting towards positive solutions.

I was fortunate to have a support group that embodied this approach, led by a therapist who truly understood this. They acknowledged our struggles but focused on empowering us with solutions. This made all the difference in rebuilding my life. By surrounding myself with people who understood my journey yet encouraged growth, I was able to break free from the negativity that often accompanies trauma and stigma.

### How to Distance Yourself from Negativity Without Guilt

Distancing yourself from toxic influences can trigger waves of guilt—especially if your history includes environments where conflict avoidance was a survival strategy, or where loyalty to peers and family remained paramount despite destructive behaviors. Yet, healthy boundaries are indispensable for safeguarding your mental health, fueling your motivation, and ultimately supporting your growth. This process begins by clearly identifying which behaviors or attitudes you refuse to accept, then communicating those boundaries with respect but unwavering firmness.

## 4.2  Releasing Old, Destructive Habits

Our day-to-day behaviors, often performed on autopilot, are like threads in the tapestry of who we become. Over time, these routines shape our identity—sometimes working in our favor, and sometimes reinforcing cycles we're desperate to leave behind, such as substance use, negative self-talk, or behaviors that led to legal entanglements. In this section, we explore the power of habits and how they influence self-perception, examine scientific insights on dismantling destructive patterns, and discover ways to introduce new, empowering alternatives that push us toward a more hopeful future.

Many individuals navigating reentry after incarceration or recovering from profound loss find themselves contending not just with external obstacles—like job market discrimination or housing instability—but also with deeply embedded routines that reflect survival modes rather than growth. By learning to recognize these habits and replacing them with positive ones, it becomes possible to script a new narrative of self-worth and achievement.

## How Your Habits Create Your Identity

Habits act as quiet architects of our identity, constructing the framework that dictates daily life. Every repetitive action—from how you approach breakfast each morning to the nighttime ritual winding down the day—informs the story you tell yourself about who you are. Aristotle famously wrote:

*"We are what we repeatedly do. Excellence, then, is not an act, but a habit."*

This timeless idea resonates across generations: the practices you consistently uphold become the blueprint for your character, regardless of your past circumstances.

## A Simple Habit's Ripple Effect

Research in habit formation, including studies by Dr. Wendy Wood at the University of Southern California, underscores that 40–45% of our daily actions are habitual rather than consciously chosen. This figure highlights the immense impact these automatic behaviors wield in shaping identity. If the default mode each day is laced with destructive patterns—staying up until dawn reliving past regrets, ignoring opportunities for self-improvement—then that identity continues to revolve around self-sabotage or stagnation. Conversely, building positive habits, no matter how small, rewires daily life into a purposeful endeavor.

## How Habits Fuse with Identity

Each habit nurtured—be it journaling fears, connecting with a supportive peer group, or simply hydrating consistently—contributes to the broader mosaic of who you are becoming. Thoughts, emotions, and behaviors intertwine, laying a path toward growth. For someone who believed they'd never escape a label like "offender," replacing old, destructive routines with new ones signals both inner transformation and a readiness to pursue fresh possibilities.

Embracing better habits also realigns the brain's narrative of self. In the process, destructive impulses have less room to thrive, and a redefined identity emerges—one ready to stand firm despite past mistakes, ongoing legal obligations, or the uphill battle to rebuild trust within a community. By focusing on small, constructive routines, you reinforce a self-image built on intention rather than old conditioning. Over time, these deliberate, everyday choices propel you toward the person you aspire to be.

## The Science of Breaking Bad Habits

Breaking bad habits is rooted in understanding how our behaviors operate within reinforced neural circuits, particularly in the basal ganglia. This process is shaped by repetition over time, aligning with Charles Duhigg's concept of the cue-routine-reward loop. This loop explains why certain behaviors become almost automatic.

## Understanding the Cue-Routine-Reward Loop

The cue-routine-reward loop is a powerful framework for understanding habits. It consists of three components:

1. **Cue:** This is the trigger that sets off the habit. It could be a specific time of day, a certain environment, or an emotional state.

2. **Routine:** This is the behavior that follows the cue. It's the action you take in response to the trigger.

3. **Reward:** This is the payoff or benefit you receive from the routine. It's what reinforces the behavior and makes it stick.

For example, if you always check social media when you feel stressed (cue), the routine is scrolling through your feeds, and the reward is the temporary escape from stress. By understanding these components, you can begin to disrupt and change the loop.

## Harnessing Neuroplasticity for Change

Modern neuroscience offers optimism through the concept of neuroplasticity. While Chapter 2 explored how neuroplasticity can be used to rewire your brain for success, here we focus on its application in breaking bad habits. Neuroplasticity reveals that even long-standing patterns are not irreversibly ingrained. With focused effort, new neural pathways can replace old routines, allowing individuals to reshape daily habits once considered permanent.

This process doesn't happen overnight; it emerges through continuous, mindful practice that gradually remodels your cognitive landscape. By applying this principle, you can systematically analyze the cues and rewards behind your habits and make small changes to disrupt them.

## Overcoming Chronic Procrastination

To overcome chronic procrastination, you need to systematically analyze the cues—like checking social media whenever a stressful task appears—and the rewarding sense of "temporary escape" that comes afterward. By creating small changes in your environment, such as disabling certain notifications or doing a one-minute task immediately upon each cue, progress can emerge in surprising ways. Productivity will climb, and the mental heaviness once triggered by looming deadlines will subside.

## Replacing Destructive Habits with Empowering Ones

As you dismantle old, self-defeating patterns—whether they stem from unresolved anger, entrenched procrastination, or harmful coping strategies—the next step is deliberately substituting them with habits that fortify your long-term aims. This process isn't about erasing your past but about redirecting energy into routines that align with your values, aspirations, and new understanding of yourself. The crucial element is to select alternatives that feel both meaningful and manageable.

## Shifting from Procrastination to Purpose

If you're prone to procrastination  especially if life on the outside post incarceration or the emotional weight of reentry often leaves you feeling paralyzed—try tackling the most daunting task at the start of each day. One individual, struggling to reclaim a sense of control amidst parole meetings and community service obligations, adopted this approach by waking up early and addressing one high-priority concern before the distractions of the day set in. This small, consistent change didn't just boost productivity; it fostered a renewed confidence. Confronting difficult tasks head-on helped transform anxiety over new challenges—like job applications or educational forms—into actionable steps that built momentum.

## Anchoring Empowering Habits in Your Routine

To make these empowering habits truly stick, consider weaving them into a broader daily ritual that supports overall well-being—physical, mental, and emotional. Some people find value in starting each morning with a short mindfulness practice or a list of "micro-goals" that need attention. Others conduct a weekly review, measuring progress on reentry goals, therapy milestones, or skill-building activities. By consistently pairing your new habits with structures that celebrate your achievements, you embed them more deeply into your identity.

When combined, these practices form a supportive system that undergirds each small step forward. Each positive habit you nurture, no matter how modest, reinforces the message that you're willing to make productive choices for yourself. Over time, the puzzle pieces of these daily wins coalesce into a clear picture of empowerment, pushing you toward personal growth and sustainable success.

## 4.3 Creating a Positive and Growth-Oriented Environment

Our surroundings have a profound impact on how we think, feel, and aspire. The space you inhabit can either bolster your resilience or quietly undermine it. This chapter explores how physical and mental environments intertwine—why clearing clutter frees your mind, and how intentionally designing your surroundings fosters the momentum needed to rebuild confidence and realize your goals.

For individuals grappling with system-imposed limitations, such as strict probation constraints or financial barriers, transforming their living space can offer a newfound sense of control. When everything outside feels dictated by external rules or court orders, creating a personal haven becomes a self-affirming choice—a tangible way to reaffirm your autonomy. Research in environmental psychology confirms that even subtle changes—adding natural light, softening noise levels, removing clutter—can significantly reduce stress and heighten mental clarity.

### How Your Surroundings Impact Your Mindset

Organized, thoughtfully curated spaces boost concentration and lower stress. Cluttered areas, by contrast, frequently mirror (and magnify) mental chaos. It's like an office crammed with paper piles or a shared transitional housing unit scattered with unclaimed belongings—each day in such an environment reinforces an undercurrent of overwhelm. In psychological terms, visual disorder can drain emotional energy and stall forward progress, a phenomenon that has lasting implications for those already juggling the weight of returning to society or forging a brand-new path after a devastating event.

As urban planner Jan Gehl notes, "The quality of the spaces we inhabit is inseparable from the quality of our lives." This statement resonates deeply with those seeking personal reinvention post-conviction or post-trauma: by shaping your environment, you lay a practical foundation for self-improvement. Replacing crowded, negative surroundings with elements that invite calm— like open shelves, a plant near the window, or even a small inspirational quote on the wall—reinforces an internal shift. Over time, these environmental tweaks align your outer space with the narrative of growth and possibility you're crafting.

## My Personal Journey

In my own life, creating a positive environment has been a challenging yet transformative journey. Early in my probation, I faced one of the most difficult periods when my mother was diagnosed with terminal cancer. We were living together, and I had to adapt to the demands of her care while navigating the strict parameters of my probation. The eventual loss of my mother, the foundation of my support system, left me with compounding grief. My home environment declined as a result, reflecting the turmoil I felt inside.

However, as I began to reprogram my mind and craft a new narrative, I realized that my environment needed to change to keep up with the new, restored version of myself. I started making small, manageable changes—removing daily triggers that added stress and adding reminders of my progress. These outward transformations echoed inward, fortifying a mindset geared toward renewal. My environment was no longer a reflection of my despair but a symbol of my growth.

## Practical Steps to Transform Your Environment

To make your environment an ally in your journey, rebuild by doing the following:

1. **Start Small:** Begin with one manageable change at a time. This could be clearing a cluttered area or adding a plant to your space.

2. **Identify Triggers:** Remove daily triggers that add stress or anxiety.

3. **Add Positive Reminders:** Incorporate elements that remind you of your progress and goals, such as inspirational quotes or photos.

4. **Create a Calm Space:** Use natural light, soft colors, and soothing sounds to create a calming atmosphere.

By transforming your environment, you can reinforce a mindset geared toward growth and renewal. Remember, these changes don't require elaborate renovations; sometimes, it's the small, intentional adjustments that make the biggest difference.

## The Power of Decluttering

Decluttering involves more than just tidying up; it's a crucial shift that mirrors clearing your mind. When your physical environment is chaotic, it often reflects emotional or cognitive clutter that can overwhelm your focus. The physical act of "letting go" can pave the way for re-examining old mental scripts—including deep-seated resentments or limiting beliefs—and discarding them in favor of openness and forward momentum.

## A Window into the Power of Decluttering

Individuals transitioning out of incarceration or confronting the aftermath of severe trauma often describe a profound sense of relief after reorganizing their living spaces. For example, clearing unneeded paperwork, such as old reminders of court dates or fines, can instill renewed motivation. The physical cleanup becomes symbolic: as the clutter disappears, so too does the shame and anxiety that clung to it. This process helps close the chapter on past burdens, unlocking mental space for better pursuits.

## Expert Endorsements and the Science of Letting Go

Renowned tidying expert Marie Kondo suggests a mindful approach to organizing: keep only the items that "spark joy." Her philosophy underscores that physical objects carry emotional weight, and by letting go of what no longer serves you—be it an item or an unproductive belief—you invite clarity and possibility. Similarly, mental-health professionals often recommend journaling to identify and release inner clutter: the persistent fears, negative self-talk, or unresolved anger that crowd your internal space.

Studies in cognitive and environmental psychology reveal that a clean, orderly environment tends to reduce stress and increase concentration. This is particularly vital if you're juggling systemic hurdles like restricted housing options or strict parole or probation requirements that can magnify daily stressors. Taking charge of your immediate surroundings becomes a tangible act of self-empowerment, signaling that while external constraints exist, you retain control over at least one aspect of life—your personal domain.

## Creating Room for Growth

Ultimately, the process of decluttering—physical or mental—fosters an environment conducive to a thriving, growth-oriented mindset. Clearing out old items or journaling unproductive thoughts might feel challenging at first, especially if your history involves trauma or repeated rejections. But each object discarded, each harmful notion set aside, affirms that you're free to craft a new narrative and create a space—both literal and metaphorical—that supports personal evolution.

## Designing an Environment That Supports Success

After discarding what no longer serves you—whether physical clutter, negative influences, or stagnating routines—the next natural step is to intentionally shape your surroundings so they bolster your ambitions. This involves deliberate decisions about how your space looks and feels, emphasizing positivity, focus, and an inviting sense of possibility. Simple elements like natural light, soothing colors, and well-organized furnishings can profoundly influence your motivation.

## 4.4 Setting Boundaries and Protecting Your Energy

Boundaries serve as invisible lines that safeguard your emotional and mental well-being. If you've survived incarceration, are working to repair harm you once caused, or are healing from life-altering grief, boundaries become more than a convenience—they're essential. Without them, your energy can be swept away by external demands, toxic relationships, and self-imposed obligations. By establishing clear limits, you protect your vitality and construct a strong foundation for flourishing across all areas of life.

### Why Boundaries Are Necessary for Growth

Imagine a tender plant trying to thrive in an environment where it's subjected to harsh weather, inconsistent watering, or invasive weeds. Even the most resilient plant will wither without protective structure. In much the same way, boundaries serve as defining frameworks for your well-being, ensuring that the energy you invest goes into pursuits that nourish growth rather than drain resources.

Studies in psychology and behavioral science highlight a direct relationship between well-defined personal boundaries and increased satisfaction, emotional health, and even professional performance. For individuals transitioning out of incarceration or trauma, the ability to set boundaries can be especially transformative. For example, you may experience repeated requests for help—though well-intentioned—that could wear you out and leave you unable to focus on your own rehabilitation. Recognizing this pattern, you can begin to respectfully decline obligations that clash with your personal goals. In doing so, you can funnel your renewed energy into vital steps like stable employment, therapy, and family reconnection.

Renowned researcher Dr. Brené Brown insists, *"Daring to set boundaries is about having the courage to love ourselves, even when we risk disappointing others."* Setting boundaries affirms that your time and emotional energy carry value. It allows you to direct yourself toward endeavors that truly align with your sense of purpose—be it completing a vocational program, earning back trust in a damaged relationship, or engaging with advocacy groups that promote second chances. As soon as boundaries are in place, you may find a deeper commitment to the tasks that matter, less fatigue, and a greater sense of direction. Over time, that clear sense of self-determination fosters the confidence needed to transcend whatever limitations society, or your past, may impose.

## Mastering the Art of Saying No Without Guilt

One of the most challenging aspects of setting boundaries is learning to say no without feeling guilty. Societal pressures often equate refusal with selfishness or betrayal, but in reality, asserting your limits is an act of self-respect. It protects your time, conserves emotional energy, and fosters a sense of balance that can be crucial when juggling reentry obligations, family responsibilities, or ongoing personal healing.

A practical way to develop this skill is by starting small. If someone asks you to take on an additional task, deliver a concise, genuine response: "I appreciate you thinking of me, but I have to focus on my current commitments first." This kind of honest, courteous decline clarifies your boundaries without dismissing the other person's situation.

## The Cost of Missing Boundaries

In my own life, I've learned the importance of setting boundaries the hard way. My inability to say no and establish limits led to a situation that ultimately resulted in allegations of misconduct. What began as emotional support for a student evolved into an emotional dynamic that quickly spiraled beyond my ability to control. I cared deeply for her well-being and still do, acknowledging not only the impact this had on her but also the trauma we both experienced when those allegations surfaced.

Through years of therapy and self-reflection post-conviction, I came to understand the deeper forces at play in my decision-making. While I take full responsibility for crossing a line that should never have been crossed, I also recognize now what was happening subconsciously that led to those choices and outcomes. I had spent my life conditioned to be a pushover, conflict-averse, and afraid to assert myself, and I had never learned how to set healthy, firm boundaries—especially in emotionally charged situations.

At the root of this was a "freeze" response—an ingrained survival instinct that took over whenever I felt powerless. In moments where I felt I had no way out, especially when emotions escalated quickly, I didn't take control. I didn't set limits. I simply went with the flow, as if I were at the mercy of a rushing river. Freezing had been my coping mechanism, my way of surviving. This realization was profound, particularly when I looked back at my past experiences with trauma, including a date rape where I had also frozen. For years, I had blamed myself for not saying no more forcefully, as if my silence equated to consent. It wasn't until my therapist explained that freezing is a deeply ingrained survival response, not a choice, that I finally understood what had been happening beneath the surface. I wasn't weak—I was trying to survive.

But survival isn't the same as making empowered choices. Understanding the cost of this conditioning opened my eyes to the power of boundaries. I began to recognize how much my inability to assert myself had shaped my life's trajectory. Power dynamics are not always what they seem—and sometimes, the person with legal authority is not necessarily the one in control. I now understand that even as "the adult in the room," I was still operating from a place of learned powerlessness, making me vulnerable to a situation where I was not the one calling the shots. That in no way absolves my responsibility, but it does shed light on the hidden patterns that contributed to my choices.

As someone who has been both victimized and labeled as an offender, I see now how both experiences stemmed from the same underlying issue: negative conditioning and a lack of self-preservation boundaries. I had spent my life trying to avoid conflict, accommodate others, and make people feel safe, all while never fully understanding that I wasn't keeping myself safe in the process.

That is the true cost of unexamined patterns—and it's a cost I don't want anyone else to have to pay.

## The Power of Finding Your Inner Voice

This painful truth robbed me of building anything meaningful in my life for years, but now I am equipped with the knowledge that saying "no" is an act of kindness to myself. It allows me to be the best version of myself and more capable of helping others when it's appropriate to say yes.

This journey has taught me that finding your inner voice and strength to stand your ground is crucial. It's not about blame or right and wrong; it's about understanding the power of boundaries in healing and growth.

### Practical Steps to Mastering "No"

To develop this skill, decide on incorporating the following:

1. **Start Small:** Begin with small, low-stakes situations where saying no feels manageable.

2. **Practice Assertive Communication:** Use phrases like "I appreciate your request, but I need to prioritize my commitments."

3. **Understand Your Boundaries:** Reflect on what you are and are not comfortable with.

4. **Reframe "No" as a Positive Choice:** View saying no as a way to preserve your resources for what truly matters.

By learning to say "no" without guilt, you strengthen your ability to invest in what truly matters—whether that's mental health, steady employment, or family reconnection.

## Cutting Ties with Toxic Influences

Sometimes, safeguarding your mental and emotional energy requires more than establishing boundaries—it calls for making the difficult choice to fully disengage from influences that consistently drain you. These damaging forces might be particular individuals, entire social circles, or even ingrained behaviors that perpetuate negativity and stall your forward momentum. Removing yourself from these influences is both a self-preserving and empowering act, reaffirming that you deserve an environment conducive to growth rather than harm.

**Not everything you carry from childhood belongs to you.** You didn't choose the trauma, the hurt, or the chaos you experienced growing up—but you do have a choice now. Recognizing that your past isn't your fault is vital; understanding that your future belongs to you is life-changing. Overcoming childhood victimization means consciously deciding to break free from the emotional ties that bind you to old wounds, including those negative environments and toxic influences you might have been exposed to or raised in. By reclaiming your narrative, you step into your true power, finally becoming the author of your own story.

## Real-World Resilience: Jaycee Dugard's Journey to Freedom

At just eleven years old, Jaycee Dugard was kidnapped near her home in South Lake Tahoe, California, and held captive for eighteen harrowing years. During that time, Jaycee faced extreme emotional abuse, manipulation, and psychological imprisonment, conditions that could have trapped her permanently in victimhood and trauma.

Yet Jaycee chose courage over captivity. After her rescue, she actively confronted the deeply ingrained toxic beliefs and fears instilled by her captors. Through intensive self-reflection and healing, she reclaimed her identity, overcame the lasting effects of her trauma, and transformed her experiences into meaningful advocacy.

Today, Jaycee Dugard is a bestselling author and founder of the JAYC Foundation, an organization supporting survivors of severe trauma and empowering them to rebuild their lives. Her story proves that even after the most profound victimization, it's possible to break free, reclaim your voice, and create a life defined by strength and purpose.

Jaycee's powerful journey teaches us that no situation is too dark to escape, no mindset too ingrained to change.

## Evidence from Social and Psychological Research

Studies on social networks and mental health confirm that our closest relationships hold considerable power over our emotional stability, motivation, and overall productivity. Consistent exposure to negativity or cynicism can erode confidence and even hinder compliance with crucial personal or legal milestones—whether it's showing up to counseling sessions or managing financial restitutions. By deliberately distancing yourself from corrosive influences, you claim control over your social environment, forging a circle that values and accelerates your transformation.

Leadership expert Simon Sinek observes, *"You can't influence what you don't acknowledge."*

Recognizing the toll that toxic individuals, groups, or habits impose is the starting point for building a healthier, growth-focused ecosystem. This willingness to break away isn't about casting others aside without consideration; it's about acknowledging that your emotional resilience and practical well-being must come first. When you choose relationships aligned with healing and hope, you reinforce your own capacity for reinvention—a critical step if you're navigating life after criminal justice involvement, recovering from a deep personal crisis, or charting a brand-new direction for your future.

# Chapter 4 Case Study: Susan Burton

## Background:

Susan Burton was born and raised in the housing projects of East Los Angeles, California. Her early life was marked by turmoil and instability, leading to significant personal challenges. In 1982, tragedy struck when her five-year-old son, Marque Hamilton, was accidentally killed by a police cruiser. Overwhelmed by grief and lacking access to professional support, Burton turned to drugs and alcohol, eventually becoming addicted to crack cocaine. This addiction led to a cycle of incarceration throughout the 1980s and 1990s, as she was repeatedly arrested and jailed for nonviolent drug-related offenses in Los Angeles County.

Application of Principles:

- **Identifying Toxic Influences:** Burton recognized that her environment and the unresolved trauma from her son's death were perpetuating her addiction and incarceration. Acknowledging these toxic influences was the first step toward change.

- **Releasing Destructive Habits:** Determined to break free from her addiction, Burton sought help from the CLARE Foundation in Santa Monica, California, in 1997. This decision marked the beginning of her journey toward sobriety and personal transformation.

- **Creating a Positive Environment:** After achieving sobriety, Burton founded A New Way of Life Reentry Project in 1998. This nonprofit organization provides housing and support to formerly incarcerated women, offering a nurturing environment that fosters recovery and reintegration into society.

- **Setting Boundaries and Protecting Energy:** Through her organization, Burton established a community where women could support each other while maintaining boundaries that promote personal growth and prevent relapse into old patterns.

## Outcome:

Susan Burton's dedication to breaking free from toxic patterns and environments has led to significant personal and community achievements. Her organization has provided housing to over 1,200 women and children, reunited more than 400 women with their children, and offered pro bono legal services to assist over 3,000 individuals seeking relief from the burden of criminal histories. Her memoir, *Becoming Ms. Burton: From Prison to Recovery to Leading the Fight for Incarcerated Women*, received the 2018 NAACP Image Award for Outstanding Literary Work in the category of Biography/Autobiography. Burton's story exemplifies the power of resilience and the impact of creating supportive environments for those seeking to transform their lives after incarceration.

## 4.5 Action Plan – Detox Your Life for Success

Visualize living without the weight of negativity—a future where harmful relationships, unproductive habits, and draining environments are consciously replaced with supportive, nurturing influences. This plan offers a practical blueprint for that transformation, starting with an "Energy Audit" to identify your main energy drains, transitioning into daily mental detox practices, and culminating in building a high-vibration support system.

### Weekly Detox Plan

1. **Energy Audit (30 minutes):**
   - Begin by listing people, activities, or recurring thoughts that leave you feeling depleted. Document these observations to reveal patterns that could go unnoticed amidst day-to-day struggles.
   - Ask yourself which of these factors stand directly in the way of your bigger goals.

2. **Identify and Limit Energy Drains (30 minutes):**
   - **Examine any recurring themes:** Is it a coworker's relentless

pessimism, a roommate's chaotic lifestyle, or your own habit of doomscrolling each morning?

- Decide whether to limit exposure, adjust circumstances, or, when necessary, make deeper cuts.

3. **Daily Mental Detox (15 minutes):**

- Engage in daily practices that cleanse your mind of negativity. This could be meditation, journaling, or simply taking a few minutes to focus on your breath.

- Use this time to reflect on your progress and reinforce positive thoughts.

4. **Build a High-Vibration Support Network (60 minutes):**

- Review your existing connections—ask which individuals fortify your positive momentum and which ones consistently bring you down.

- Limit contact with those who perpetuate negativity and seek out communities that share your values and aspirations.

5. **Weekly Reflection and Adjustment (30 minutes):**

- Reflect on your progress each week. Identify areas where you've improved and where you still need to work.

- Adjust your plan based on your reflections, ensuring it remains aligned with your goals.

## Monthly Challenge

- **Implement One Major Change:** Choose one significant energy drain to address each month. Develop a plan to minimize its impact and take consistent action towards removing it.

- **Share Your Progress:** Share your progress with a trusted friend or mentor. This can help keep you accountable and motivated.

### Additional Strategies for Success

1. **Surround Yourself with Positivity:** Engage in activities that uplift you, such as reading inspiring stories or listening to motivational podcasts.

2. **Practice Gratitude:** Reflect daily on things you are grateful for. This helps shift your focus from negativity to positivity.

3. **Set Boundaries:** Learn to say no to requests that drain your energy and yes to those that support your goals.

4. **Celebrate Small Wins:** Acknowledge and celebrate each small victory along the way. This helps build confidence and reinforces positive behaviors.

By following this action plan, you'll begin to detox your life, replacing negativity with supportive influences that align with your goals for success. Remember, transformation is a journey, and every small step counts.

## Chapter 4 Summary: Breaking Free from Toxic Patterns and Negative Environments

Breaking free from toxic patterns and negative environments is one of the most powerful steps you can take toward lasting transformation. In this chapter, you identified the hidden forces that have drained your energy—whether toxic people, destructive habits, or environments that keep you stuck in old cycles. You learned that your relationships, routines, and surroundings are not just background details—they actively shape your future success.

By recognizing the toxic influences holding you back, you gained the ability to set boundaries that protect your energy, reprogram negative habits, and cultivate an environment that supports your growth. These shifts aren't just about removing negativity—they're about intentionally designing a life that fuels your highest potential. Every habit you break, every space you declutter, and every boundary you enforce is a declaration that your well-being and success matter.

But recognizing and eliminating toxic influences is only half the battle. The next step is building the discipline to stay on the path of transformation.

In Chapter 5, you'll learn how to master self-discipline and unstoppable productivity—because success isn't about motivation alone, it's about creating a structure that makes growth automatic. You'll discover how to eliminate procrastination, develop laser-sharp focus, and build powerful routines that keep you moving forward, even when motivation fades.

# Chapter 5

# Mastering Self-Discipline and Unstoppable Productivity

*"Discipline is choosing between what you want now and what you want most."* – Abraham Lincoln

Success isn't just a matter of chance or raw talent; often, it's about maintaining the discipline needed to sustain focus and action. This chapter delves into the science of self-discipline and offers concrete strategies to eliminate procrastination. By understanding the brain's wiring and adopting daily practices, you can convert momentary bursts of willpower into a long-term productive engine, all while navigating the complexities of reentry, healing from trauma, or facing systemic hurdles.

## Preview – Meet Marchell Taylor

Imagine discovering in prison that your greatest barrier was something you had no control over—a brain injury affecting your behavior and choices. Marchell Taylor faced exactly this realization, yet he refused to be defined or limited by it. Marchell harnessed the power of self-discipline and commitment to productivity, transforming his disability into a powerful force for good. His story shows us how mastering discipline can turn even our greatest challenges into stepping stones.

Marchell's full transformation is detailed at the chapter's end, showing exactly how discipline became his key to freedom.

# 5.1 The Science Behind Self-Discipline

Self-discipline frequently gets mistaken for sheer willpower—the ability to push through difficult tasks no matter how drained you feel. Modern research, however, paints a more nuanced picture: discipline is both a resource and a skill. Learning to replenish and structure it effectively becomes critical, especially for individuals striving to overcome a crisis and build stable ground for the future.

## Why Willpower Alone Is a Limited Resource

Willpower, much like a muscle, tires out after sustained effort. Psychological studies indicate that our capacity for self-control fluctuates throughout the day. Early in the morning, determination might be strong, but decision fatigue creeps in as hours pass—making it harder to resist temptation or tackle unpleasant tasks. Research underscores that willpower is finite—without strategies to preserve and replenish it, even well-laid plans can unravel. Recognizing this inherent limitation is the first step toward designing a more reliable approach to discipline.

## The Real Secret to Making Discipline Effortless

If relying solely on willpower feels akin to running a marathon without fueling, the secret to consistent discipline lies in creating an environment that reduces the need for nonstop self-control. The goal is to set up your daily life so that correct actions become almost automatic. Pre-committing to your goals—like scheduling specific study times for a GED program, or placing job application materials in a neatly organized spot—eliminates the need for constant decisions. In *The Power of Habit*, Charles Duhigg explains that altering habits hinges less on brute-forcing your impulses and more on designing surroundings that make the right choices straightforward. By proactively shaping your environment, you conserve your willpower for critical moments, releasing you from perpetual self-battle.

## How to Rewire Your Brain for Delayed Gratification

Cultivating a mindset that embraces delayed gratification is essential for long-term success. This involves training your brain to appreciate future rewards more than fleeting satisfactions. Breaking bigger goals into smaller, milestone-based tasks provides consistent markers of progress, reinforcing patience. For example, if you struggle with frequent urges to check social media, devised a plan: set a simple timer for 30-minute work intervals, permitting a short break only after completing each session. Over time, your brain will start associating focused work with an uplifting sense of reward—a cycle that fosters steady productivity even in the face of legal limitations or emotional burdens.

Neuroscience backs this process. Studies show the prefrontal cortex—the area overseeing planning and self-control—can be strengthened through repeated acts of delaying gratification. Dr. Walter Mischel's renowned "marshmallow test" directly links self-control abilities to improved life outcomes. Training yourself to prioritize distant benefits over immediate temptations not only elevates productivity but also establishes a firm bedrock of resilience. This is especially critical for those building a new chapter after convictions, personal tragedies, or socio-economic setbacks. As these neural pathways evolve, you develop the discipline necessary to stay focused, effectively bridging the gap between short-term desires and the larger vision that will define your future success.

Andre Norman spent 14 years incarcerated, including a period in solitary confinement. Recognizing that lack of discipline led him down a negative path, he dedicated himself to a strict routine focused on education, behavioral reform, and personal responsibility. Upon release, Andre leveraged his disciplined habits to become an international speaker, author, and Harvard Fellow, mentoring others to develop productive habits, structure, and personal accountability.

### Real-World Resilience: J.K. Rowling's Disciplined Rise from Rock Bottom

In her late twenties, J.K. Rowling was struggling as a single mother living in near poverty. Recently divorced, grieving her mother's death, unemployed, and battling severe depression, Rowling felt trapped in a cycle of hopelessness. Yet, even during these dark times, she clung to one daily practice: writing.

Rowling committed herself to disciplined productivity, regularly writing pages of a story in small cafés and while riding trains around Edinburgh. Despite numerous rejections from publishers, Rowling persisted, driven by relentless self-discipline and a deep belief in her vision. Her discipline and productivity eventually paid off—those daily writing sessions became the beloved *"Harry Potter"* series, transforming her from struggling single mother to one of the world's most successful authors.

J.K. Rowling's extraordinary story teaches us that true productivity and lasting success come from mastering self-discipline, even—and especially—when the path ahead seems impossible.

# 5.2 Destroying Procrastination and Taking Massive Action

Procrastination acts like a silent thief, stealing valuable hours and limiting your potential. It can sabotage even the most determined plans. Let's explore why we postpone tasks, outline strategies to spark momentum with the simple yet powerful "5-Minute Rule," and emphasize accountability structures to ensure you keep taking massive, consistent action.

### Why We Procrastinate and How to Overcome It

Procrastination is rarely about laziness; it usually reflects a tangled mix of fear, perfectionism, and the burden of potential criticism. When faced with uncertain outcomes—like seeking a new job despite a prior conviction or resuming education after personal hardship—the mind can freeze in anticipation of failure or judgment. Research in behavioral psychology indicates that procrastination functions as a coping mechanism, helping us avoid the emotional discomfort tied to challenging tasks.

With honest self-reflection, you can understand that the fear fueling delay isn't about skill or ability; it's about the dread of not meeting personal or external expectations. Breaking down the paperwork into smaller steps and setting realistic benchmarks transformed hesitation into forward movement. As motivational speaker Brian Tracy reminds us, *"Successful people are simply those with successful habits."*

Acknowledging that fear drives much of our procrastination helps dismantle the inner dialogue that keeps us stuck, while setting more achievable milestones fosters a sense of control and progress.

## The "5-Minute Rule" for Instant Momentum

Often the toughest hurdle in any undertaking is simply starting. The "5-Minute Rule" offers a direct remedy: commit to working on a task for just five minutes. This minimal promise is often enough to overcome the initial blockade and generate a small but essential sense of accomplishment, fueling you to keep going.

Have you ever had a task so daunting, the scope of it felt overwhelming, triggering a cycle of avoidance? Embracing the "5-Minute Rule," you can set a timer and begin tackling the task—and what you'll find is that once the first steps are taken, the resistance softs. This modest action can become a springboard to sustain focus and gradually dispel that sense of impossibility. Neuroscientific studies highlight how the brain experiences a "reward" when you commence a task, reinforcing the behavior and making it simpler to continue. In essence, the smallest step—just five minutes—can break the chains of inaction and open the door to measurable progress.

## Creating Accountability to Guarantee Action

Accountability is often the key factor distinguishing wishful thinking from actual results. By publicly declaring your goals or aligning with a supportive group, you establish a dynamic that *pressures* you—in a constructive way—to follow through. Accountability can involve forming a buddy system with a friend pursuing similar milestones, attending a weekly reentry support group, or even using a digital platform where you log daily achievements.

In my weekly therapy group, we would share obstacles faced and offer solution-focused feedback. This mutual responsibility led to more consistent dedication, reinforcing each person's commitment despite hurdles like the emotional toll of past failures. Research in social psychology confirms that having an accountability structure heightens persistence and performance by adding a layer of external validation that complements one's internal drive.

In addition, consider personal rituals—like a daily reflection session—to track accomplishments and set fresh targets. Such habits serve a dual purpose: they celebrate progress, however small, and clarify next steps for tomorrow. By knitting accountability into your daily or weekly routine, you create a solid framework that turns ideas into tangible victories—a vital transition if you're determined to break free from cycles of avoidance and harness your potential for a more dynamic, fulfilling life.

## Harnessing Neuroplasticity for Success Across Neurodiverse Brains

Becoming aware of how your brain functions is incredibly important, especially for individuals on the autism spectrum or those with ADHD. Neuroplasticity offers a powerful tool for adapting and thriving, regardless of how your brain is wired.

## Understanding Executive Function and Neurodiversity

Executive function, which includes skills like planning, organization, and self-regulation, can vary significantly across individuals. For those on the autism spectrum or with ADHD, executive function challenges might manifest differently. It's crucial to recognize these differences and leverage strategies that work in harmony with your unique brain function.

## My Personal Journey with ADHD

I wasn't diagnosed with ADHD until I was 32—after my arrest, when I finally began therapy. At first, the diagnosis hit me like a wave of frustration and regret, launching me into a spiral of "what if" questions I couldn't escape. *What if I had known earlier? Would I have even pursued teaching? Would medication have helped me make different choices—choices that could have prevented me from ever crossing that line with my former student? Could all of this have been avoided if I had just understood myself better?*

I never struggled with focus in school, and I had successfully completed my degree programs, so it never occurred to me that I might have ADHD. But my symptoms didn't show up the way I had always thought ADHD looked. Instead of inattention, I experienced intense emotions and impulsivity, especially in heightened emotional situations. My decisions weren't coming from a place of recklessness, but from a brain wired for urgency—acting first, processing later.

At first, the diagnosis felt like just another label—another sentence being imposed on me. I had already been judged, already been defined by my worst mistake, and now I had something else that made me feel different, broken, or defective. But over time, I realized that this wasn't a punishment—it was information. Information that could help me understand myself, recognize my patterns, and, most importantly, give me the tools to work with my brain instead of feeling like I was constantly fighting against it.

## Empowering Yourself with Awareness and Tools

Once I committed to learning about my brain and recognizing when I was operating in a hyper-emotional state, I began to develop tools and techniques to work with my executive functioning. This newfound awareness allowed me to reprogram my responses and not let my limitations dictate my success. By acknowledging, honoring, and adapting to my neurodiverse brain, I was able to overcome challenges that once seemed insurmountable, particularly, regulating my emotions.

## Strategies for Neurodiverse Success

Here are some strategies that can help individuals with ADHD or on the autism spectrum harness neuroplasticity for success:

1. **Awareness and Acceptance:** The first step is acknowledging how your brain functions and accepting it. This awareness is crucial for developing strategies that work for you.

2. **Adaptive Tools and Techniques:** Use tools like planners, apps, or reminders to help with organization and time management. For emotional regulation, practices like deep breathing and yoga helped me the most.

3. **Neuroplasticity-Based Training:** Engage in activities that challenge your brain and promote neuroplasticity, such as learning a new skill or hobby. This can help strengthen executive function over time.

4. **Support Network:** Surround yourself with people who understand and support your neurodiverse needs. This can provide a safety net and help you stay motivated.

By embracing your neurodiversity and leveraging neuroplasticity, you can create a personalized path to success that aligns with your unique strengths and challenges.

# 5.3 Developing Laser-Focused Productivity

Distraction is the silent killer of ambition. In a world filled with constant notifications, endless scrolling, and competing demands for attention, the ability to focus deeply has become a rare and powerful skill. Productivity isn't just about doing more—it's about doing the right things with undivided attention. In this chapter, we explore how to eliminate distractions permanently, master time-blocking and deep work strategies, and apply the best productivity hacks used by high performers to achieve more in less time.

## How to Eliminate Distractions Permanently

Distractions aren't just external—they're internal. Many people believe that their biggest obstacle to focus is the outside world: social media, emails, or co-workers dropping by unannounced. But often, distraction originates from within. The mind seeks out stimulation when a task feels difficult, uncomfortable, or uncertain. This is why, even when we clear external interruptions, we still find ourselves mindlessly checking our phones or reorganizing our desks instead of tackling the work that truly matters.

To eliminate distractions permanently, you must address both external and internal triggers. Start with your environment—set clear boundaries for when and where deep work happens. Internally, distraction often stems from unresolved thoughts or a lack of clarity about what needs to be done. A simple yet powerful technique is the "brain dump" method: before starting deep work, take five minutes to write down every lingering thought or worry. By externalizing these mental distractions, you free up cognitive bandwidth and allow your brain to focus entirely on the task at hand.

Finally, technology should be your servant, not your master. Use tools like website blockers, phone settings that limit notifications, or even a second "distraction-free" laptop with no social media or entertainment apps installed. By systematically removing friction, you make focus your default state.

## Time-Blocking and Deep Work Strategies

The most productive people don't just work hard—they work with intention. One of the most effective ways to maximize focus is through time-blocking, a strategy where you assign specific blocks of time for deep, uninterrupted work. Instead of working reactively—jumping from one task to another as distractions arise—you proactively schedule dedicated periods for high-priority activities.

Cal Newport, author of *Deep Work*, emphasizes that deep, focused work is the ultimate competitive advantage in the modern economy. He suggests structuring your day around extended periods of concentration, free from shallow tasks like checking emails or engaging in social media. A useful rule of thumb is to schedule deep work in 90-minute sessions, followed by short breaks to reset and recharge.

For time-blocking to be effective, treat your scheduled work time as unbreakable as a meeting with a high-profile client. One strategy that transformed my own productivity was creating a "Power Hour"—a one-hour, distraction-free work session first thing in the morning before checking emails or messages. This single adjustment doubled my output and eliminated the mental fatigue of juggling competing tasks throughout the day.

Another critical element of deep work is task batching, where similar activities are grouped together to minimize cognitive switching. Instead of answering emails sporadically throughout the day, allocate a set time—say, 11 AM and 4 PM—for handling communication. Research from the American Psychological Association shows that switching between tasks can reduce productivity by as much as 40% due to the mental "reset" required each time. The fewer transitions you have, the more effective your deep work sessions will be.

## The Best Productivity Hacks for High Performers

High performers don't rely on motivation—they rely on systems. Here are some of the most effective productivity hacks that top achievers use to consistently perform at peak levels:

- **The Two-Minute Rule:** If a task takes less than two minutes to complete, do it immediately. This prevents small tasks from piling up and cluttering your to-do list.

- **The Eisenhower Matrix:** Prioritize tasks using this simple but effective framework:

    o *Urgent & Important:* Do it immediately.

    o *Important but Not Urgent:* Schedule it.

    o *Urgent but Not Important:* Delegate it.

o *Neither Urgent nor Important:* Eliminate it.

By filtering tasks through this framework, you ensure that your time is spent on what truly moves the needle.

- **Energy-Based Scheduling:** Instead of forcing yourself to complete difficult tasks when you're drained, align your work with your natural energy levels. Many high performers tackle their most challenging work during their peak mental hours—whether that's early morning or late at night.

- **The 80/20 Rule (Pareto Principle):** Focus on the 20% of tasks that generate 80% of the results. Instead of spreading yourself thin across a dozen priorities, identify the few key actions that yield the highest return and direct your energy there.

- **The "Shut-Down Ritual":** At the end of each workday, take five minutes to review what you accomplished, set your top priorities for tomorrow, and mentally "close" the workday. This helps your brain disengage and prevents lingering thoughts from creeping into your evening and affecting your rest.

## 5.4 Building a Bulletproof Morning Routine

How you start your morning determines the trajectory of your entire day. A chaotic, reactive start often leads to an unproductive, scattered mindset, whereas a structured, intentional morning creates momentum, focus, and resilience. The world's highest achievers—from CEOs to elite athletes— understand this and design their mornings to prime their minds for success. In this chapter, we explore the habits of the ultra-successful, the key principles of crafting a routine that enhances mental clarity, and a simple 20-minute practice that rewires your brain for peak performance every single day.

### The Morning Habits of the World's Most Successful People

Success leaves clues, and few things provide as much insight into a person's mindset as their morning routine. While their specific habits may vary, the most successful individuals share common patterns: they start the day with clarity, purpose, and physical movement.

One of the most well-documented morning routines belongs to Apple CEO Tim Cook, who starts his day at 4:30 AM, immediately reviewing customer feedback to stay connected to his company's mission. Oprah Winfrey, on the other hand, begins her mornings with meditation, followed by movement, setting a tone of mindfulness and energy. Meanwhile, Richard Branson prioritizes exercise and outdoor activity, using the morning hours to elevate his physical and mental state before tackling business demands.

The underlying principle is simple: successful people don't wake up and react to the day. They take control from the very first moment, ensuring they enter their most important work with clarity and momentum. Even if you don't aspire to wake up before sunrise, adopting elements of these habits can radically improve your ability to focus and execute throughout the day.

## How to Create a Routine That Primes Your Mind for Success

The key to an effective morning routine isn't complexity—it's consistency. A well-designed routine acts as a signal to your brain, preparing it for high performance. The most effective ones focus on three key areas: mental clarity, physical energy, and intentionality.

First, start with mental clarity. Before checking emails or social media, spend a few moments engaging in stillness—whether through meditation, deep breathing, or journaling. This simple practice shifts your mind from reactive mode to proactive thinking, allowing you to approach challenges with a calm and centered perspective.

Next, activate your body. Movement first thing in the morning isn't just about fitness; it's about priming your brain. Studies show that even 10 minutes of light exercise increases dopamine and serotonin levels, enhancing mood and cognitive function for hours. Whether it's stretching, yoga, or a short walk, moving your body early signals to your brain that it's time to engage with the day.

Finally, set your intentions. Take a moment to define what matters most. Ask yourself: *What is the single most important thing I need to accomplish today?* Writing this down or verbalizing it conditions your mind to prioritize meaningful work over distractions. One simple adjustment that changed my own productivity was shifting from a to-do list filled with minor tasks to identifying one or two high-impact priorities. The difference was transformational—my mornings became a launchpad rather than a checklist of small wins.

## The 20-Minute Exercise That Rewires Your Mindset Daily

If you could commit just 20 minutes each morning to a practice that sharpened your focus, increased resilience, and rewired your mindset for success, would you do it? This exercise is a powerful combination of visualization, affirmation, and intentional planning, designed to align your mind, emotions, and actions before the chaos of the day begins.

**The first five minutes:** Visualization. Close your eyes and picture your day unfolding exactly as you want it to. See yourself tackling challenges with confidence, handling unexpected obstacles with ease, and ending the day with a sense of accomplishment. Neuroscience confirms that mental rehearsal strengthens neural pathways, making success more likely by programming your brain for the outcomes you seek.

**The next five minutes:** Affirmations. Speak or write down empowering statements that reinforce the mindset you want to cultivate. Instead of passive, generic phrases, use affirmations tied to action: "I am in control of my focus and energy today," or "I create success through consistent effort and smart decisions." Research shows that affirmations, when repeated regularly, shift subconscious beliefs, leading to tangible behavior changes.

**The final ten minutes:** Intentional planning. Review your top priorities and commit to one key action that will move you closer to your biggest goal. This prevents the common trap of filling your day with low-impact tasks while avoiding the meaningful work that drives real progress. A well-defined plan, executed early, eliminates decision fatigue and builds momentum before distractions arise.

## Chapter 5 Case Study: Marchell Taylor

### Background:

Marchell Taylor, a resident of Denver, Colorado, had a tumultuous past marked by multiple convictions and substance abuse, spending more than half his life incarcerated. After only 36 days post-release, while on parole, he attempted armed robbery and was arrested again. In 2017, while awaiting trial and facing a potential 300-year sentence for multiple offenses, Taylor underwent a neuropsychological evaluation as part of a pilot mental health program led by neuropsychologist Kim Gorgens. This assessment revealed that Taylor had a traumatic brain injury (TBI) resulting from a childhood car accident, a condition that had gone undiagnosed for decades and significantly impacted his behavior and decision-making processes.

### Application of Principles:

- **Self-Awareness and Acceptance:** The diagnosis of TBI provided Taylor with a profound understanding of the underlying factors influencing his past behaviors. This self-awareness was the first step toward personal transformation, allowing him to accept his neurodivergent condition and its impact on his life choices.

- **Commitment to Rehabilitation:** With the knowledge of his TBI, Taylor engaged in tailored treatment and therapy programs designed to address his specific neurological needs. This commitment to rehabilitation required immense self-discipline and a willingness to confront and modify deeply ingrained behavioral patterns.

- **Advocacy and Mentorship:** Recognizing the prevalence of undiagnosed TBIs among incarcerated individuals, Taylor co-founded AYBOS Advocacy, an organization dedicated to providing TBI screenings and connecting affected individuals with necessary treatments. Through this initiative, he mentors others, sharing his journey to inspire and guide them toward rehabilitation and personal growth.

## Outcome:

Marchell Taylor's journey from long-term incarceration to becoming a peer counselor and advocate exemplifies the transformative power of self-discipline and productivity. His efforts have contributed to the expansion of TBI screening programs in Colorado prisons, highlighting the importance of mental health support in reducing recidivism and aiding rehabilitation. Taylor's story underscores the significant impact of addressing neurodivergent conditions within the criminal justice system and serves as a testament to the potential for personal transformation when individuals are provided with appropriate support and resources.

# 5.5 Action Plan – Daily Self-Discipline Blueprint

Self-discipline isn't an innate trait; it's a muscle that grows stronger with deliberate, daily effort. The difference between those who achieve extraordinary success and those who remain stuck in cycles of inconsistency often comes down to one thing: the ability to show up and do the work, even when motivation is absent. This action plan is designed to give you a structured, sustainable way to cultivate discipline.

## Weekly Discipline Plan

1.  **Commit to One Discipline Habit (10 minutes):**

    *   Choose one non-negotiable discipline habit—something that stretches you but remains achievable. This could be waking up at 5 AM, exercising daily, writing 500 words a day, or eliminating distractions during deep work hours.

    *   Focus on consistency rather than perfection.

2. **Escalate Your Habit (15 minutes):**
   - Each week, increase the intensity or duration of your habit. If your habit is working out, extend your sessions. If it's focused work, reduce distractions further.
   - Reflect on how these small increases impact your overall discipline.

3. **Track Resistance (10 minutes):**
   - Journal about moments when you wanted to quit and analyze your triggers. Awareness is half the battle.
   - Identify patterns and develop strategies to overcome them.

4. **Eliminate Excuses (15 minutes):**
   - Double down on execution, reinforce your progress, and refine the habit so it becomes effortless.
   - Celebrate each small victory along the way.

5. **Daily Journaling (10 minutes):**
   - **Use the following prompts to stay focused:**
     - "What is the one thing I must accomplish today?"
     - "What resistance am I feeling, and how will I push through?"
     - "What small win did I achieve today?"
   - Reflect on how these prompts help you stay accountable and reinforce your goals.

## Monthly Reflection and Adjustment

- **Assess Your Progress:** Take time to reflect on how far you've come. Identify areas where you've improved and where you still need to work.
- **Adjust Your Plan:** Based on your reflections, adjust your weekly habits to better align with your goals.

## Additional Strategies for Success

1. **Tie Discipline to Your Identity:** Instead of saying, "I'm trying to be more disciplined," say, "I am someone who follows through, no matter what." Your brain is wired to act in alignment with your identity—make discipline part of how you define yourself.

2. **Remove Decision Fatigue:** Automate discipline by eliminating unnecessary choices. Design your environment so that discipline is the default.

3. **Focus on Momentum, Not Perfection:** The key to lifelong discipline isn't flawless execution—it's showing up consistently. One missed day won't derail progress, but allowing exceptions to snowball will. Instead of aiming for streaks, aim for resilience.

By following this action plan, you'll begin to cultivate self-discipline as a lifelong habit, transforming it from a struggle into a natural part of who you are.

# Chapter 5 Summary: Mastering Self-Discipline and Unstoppable Productivity

Mastering self-discipline isn't about sheer willpower—it's about designing a life where success becomes automatic. In this chapter, you learned how to build structured habits, eliminate procrastination, and optimize your focus, so that productivity isn't something you chase—it's something you embody.

By shifting your mindset from short-term comfort to long-term success, you've taken control of your daily actions, routines, and mental energy. You now understand that discipline is not about restriction—it's about freedom. The more intentional you are with your time, focus, and habits, the more you create the life you actually want.

But self-discipline isn't just about productivity—it's also about how you manage your finances and build lasting wealth.

In Chapter 6, we'll explore financial success and the wealth mindset transformation. You'll discover how to break free from the paycheck-to-paycheck cycle, overcome limiting money beliefs, and create a financial system that builds long-term security. Because success isn't just about what you do—it's also about how you leverage the resources you have.

# Chapter 6

# Financial Success and Wealth Mindset Transformation

*"Rich people think long-term. Poor people think short-term."* – T. Harv Eker

Financial success goes far beyond income—it's about how you perceive and handle money, and ultimately how you permit it to shape your future. Many people inadvertently sabotage their financial prospects through subconscious beliefs formed in childhood or through persistent scarcity mindsets. The true difference between individuals who build wealth and those who remain caught in financial strain isn't raw intelligence or luck—it's mindset and strategy.

This chapter explores the deep-rooted programming that influences your financial decisions, reveals the limiting beliefs dictating your relationship with money, and lays the groundwork for cultivating a wealth mindset that can attract financial stability. For individuals reentering society with a history of incarceration, or rebuilding life in the wake of crisis, transforming your approach to money can mark a pivotal step from mere survival to a state of genuine progress.

## Preview – Meet Curtis "Wall Street" Carroll

Picture yourself behind prison bars at just seventeen, facing decades of confinement. Curtis Carroll, known as "Wall Street," was illiterate, broke, and hopeless. Yet within prison, he discovered something powerful—financial literacy. Curtis overcame his poverty mindset, educated himself, and became an expert on wealth-building from his prison cell. His story proves that financial success isn't reserved for the privileged; it's accessible to anyone willing to change their mindset.

Curtis's full journey is featured at the end of this chapter, showcasing the financial mindset shift that changed his life.

## 6.1 Understanding Your Money Mindset

Your money mindset functions like an invisible script, quietly guiding every financial move—whether you stash funds away or overspend impulsively, whether you invest strategically or shy away from all risk. Many of these internal narratives were established in childhood, shaping your attitudes toward wealth, success, and financial security. If your mindset is anchored in scarcity, you may find yourself constantly fearing that resources will never be enough. But if you embrace an abundance framework, opportunities may feel considerably more accessible.

Think about those who have navigated the criminal justice system, often facing financial penalties, limited job prospects, and the weight of stigma. Their underlying money mindset can be a reflection of not only childhood upbringing but also the experiences of legal debts and restrictions that reinforce scarcity. Rewriting these ingrained stories is a crucial step toward a future with more consistent, stable finances.

### How Childhood Programming Affects Your Finances

Think about the earliest messages you received around money. Did you grow up in a home where financial tension overshadowed daily life—past-due notices piling up, frequent fights about the rent? Or did you hear statements like "Money doesn't grow on trees" or "The rich only get richer"? Perhaps you witnessed parents or guardians constantly in conflict over bills, encouraging the notion that money is more a source of stress than an avenue for opportunities.

Research indicates that most financial habits are shaped by age seven, implying that the money decisions you make as an adult often trace back to those early experiences. An individual who watched caregivers struggle paycheck to paycheck might harbor a persistent dread of financial instability—even after securing a stable income. Alternatively, someone who saw money spent without caution might wrestle with budgeting or saving, mirroring a habit of reckless expenditure.

## Overcoming Childhood Conditioning

Breaking free from this early programming starts with awareness. Ask yourself:

- **What were the dominant money messages in my household?**

- **How did my parents or guardians handle money?**

- **How might those habits be influencing my financial decisions today?**

Understanding these subconscious patterns forms the foundation for reshaping them. When a person returns from incarceration, for instance, there may be old narratives—like believing employers won't pay fairly or that saving is futile. Recognizing these beliefs can lay the groundwork to adopt new behaviors: meticulously tracking expenses, learning to invest bit by bit, or associating with mentors who encourage financial discipline. By challenging dated assumptions and opening up to a new, more empowering perspective on money, you begin to dissolve the barriers that might keep you in a cycle of financial stress.

## Breaking Limiting Money Beliefs

If you feel as though financial success always slips out of reach, chances are that limiting beliefs around money are holding you back. Here are some frequent—but deeply ingrained—money myths that keep people stuck:

- **"I'm just not good with money."**

  This assumption casts financial literacy as an inborn trait, not a learnable skill. In reality, handling money effectively is a teachable process—one that countless wealthy individuals cultivated over time through reading, mentorship, and trial-and-error. They weren't born as expert investors or budgeters.

- **"I have to work harder to make more money."**

  While dedicated effort is crucial, accumulating wealth isn't exclusively about grinding long hours. Those who attain lasting prosperity often use smart strategies like passive income streams, careful investments, and leveraging assets that generate revenue without trading every hour for dollars.

- **"Money is the root of all evil."**

  This belief can unconsciously push people away from wealth because they view money as something corrupt. Yet money itself is morally neutral—it amplifies the character of the person wielding it. If generosity is part of your nature when you have little, you'll likely become more giving once you have ample resources.

## Reframing Negative Narratives

To break these beliefs, consciously replace them with empowering alternatives:

- Swap *"I'm bad with money"* for *"I am actively learning to improve my financial skills."*

- Replace *"I have to work harder for money"* with *"I find ways to make my money work for me."*

- Turn *"Money is the root of all evil"* into *"Money is a tool that can create freedom and positive impact."*

Remember, your financial reality tends to mirror what you believe is feasible. Shift your core assumptions, and your external outcomes often begin to change accordingly.

## Developing a Mindset of Financial Abundance

Transitioning from a mindset of scarcity to one of abundance involves retraining your brain to spot possibilities instead of obstacles. Scarcity thinking is anchored in fear—concerns about never having enough, anxiety over potential loss, or apprehension of a looming financial crisis. By contrast, an abundance perspective starts with confidence that resources, opportunities, and personal agency are in your favor.

## Practical Strategies for Abundance

1. **Surround Yourself with Wealth-Conscious Individuals**

   If those around you regularly express financial defeatism, it's easy to adopt similar habits. Seek out mentors, peers, or online communities who prioritize financial education, investing, and long-term wealth-building. Their outlook and practices will naturally influence you toward more constructive money behaviors.

2. **Shift from "I can't afford it" to "How can I afford it?"**

   This subtle change in language challenges your brain to find solutions rather than accept excuses. People with a wealth-oriented mentality don't stop at "no"—they explore side incomes, refine budgeting, or research clever investment strategies.

3. **Engage in Financial Gratitude**

   Instead of dwelling on what you lack, actively value the resources you already possess. Studies show that expressing gratitude not only fosters a healthier mental state but also enhances resilience. Make it a habit to acknowledge at least one financial positive each day, be it a small paycheck, an investment yield, or the capacity to settle a bill on time. Gratitude rewires your mindset toward more is possible.

An abundance mindset isn't about reckless spending or ignoring real-world constraints—it's about recognizing that financial success can be within your grasp and making targeted moves to achieve it. No matter how you are rebuilding life after personal catastrophe, learning to see money as a tool for freedom and impact propels you toward a brighter, self-directed future.

Embracing abundance and practicing gratitude can powerfully reshape your financial mindset—but let's also acknowledge that this practice can feel particularly challenging if scarcity and financial hardship have shaped your life experience. It's essential to recognize that a gratitude mindset doesn't erase the harsh realities you might be facing; rather, it empowers you to face them differently. To fully benefit from these abundance practices, we must first compassionately acknowledge the significant barriers many people face, especially those resulting from systemic poverty, generational hardship, or profound financial loss. By acknowledging these realities, you can authentically begin shifting your mindset toward financial empowerment and sustainable change.

## Understanding the Weight of Financial Devastation and Systemic Poverty

It's one thing to discuss money mindsets when you're simply trying to improve your financial habits; it's another thing entirely when financial devastation or systemic poverty has defined your entire experience of life. Many self-help books overlook the very real, heavy, and sometimes suffocating weight of poverty—particularly generational poverty, systemic barriers, and the deep emotional scars left by financial trauma.

When you've experienced profound financial loss or have grown up in poverty, money isn't just money. It represents safety, dignity, opportunity, and hope—things that, for much of your life, may have felt painfully out of reach. Perhaps you've experienced eviction, foreclosure, or the anxiety of not knowing where your next meal will come from. Maybe you grew up feeling ashamed or misunderstood, with constant reminders from society that you're "less than" simply because of your financial status.

I understand how relentless and unforgiving poverty can feel. When you're stuck in survival mode, planning for the future can seem pointless, even absurd. You're focused on getting through the day, week, or month—not dreaming about wealth. You're not lacking motivation or discipline; you're lacking resources, opportunities, and access to financial education that truly understands your situation.

But here's what you need to hear clearly: Your financial past does not have to dictate your financial future.

Financial devastation, whether due to job loss, illness, incarceration, systemic racism, or generational poverty, leaves deep emotional and psychological scars. It's normal to feel powerless, angry, or even hopeless. Yet, your path forward begins with acknowledging that although these challenges are immense, they can still be overcome. You have the power to redefine your relationship with money, not by ignoring the harsh realities you've faced, but by courageously confronting them and using proven strategies to rewrite your financial narrative.

**The Real Cost of Poverty:** Systemic poverty isn't just about lacking money—it's about lacking opportunity. It often means lower access to quality education, fewer job opportunities, poor healthcare, constant stress, and emotional exhaustion. It's a cycle that's brutally difficult to escape precisely because it's more than just financial. Overcoming systemic poverty requires addressing both internal beliefs about money and external barriers in a strategic, intentional way.

**Breaking Through Despite the Odds:** Let's look at Oprah Winfrey. Born in rural Mississippi, she experienced firsthand what it means to feel trapped by systemic poverty. Her environment suggested she should expect nothing more than survival. But Oprah chose differently. She chose to shift her mindset about money and her worth, even when she had every reason not to believe change was possible. Through sheer determination, strategic planning, and purposeful action, Oprah transformed her relationship with money and ultimately her life. Today, she's not just wealthy; she empowers millions to break free from poverty's psychological chains.

Oprah's story is powerful not because she's famous, but because she overcame genuine financial trauma by consciously and deliberately choosing to rewrite her money narrative. Her transformation didn't come easily—it required her to address deeply embedded beliefs about scarcity, worthiness, and abundance.

Your journey begins the same way—by recognizing that systemic poverty and financial trauma are real, but they are not immovable. They don't have to permanently define you.

**Moving Forward with Empathy and Strategy:** As we move forward in this chapter, we'll discuss practical, realistic strategies to escape the paycheck-to-paycheck cycle, develop financial literacy, and ultimately build genuine, sustainable wealth. These strategies acknowledge your starting point, respecting the complexity of your journey while guiding you step-by-step toward a future defined by financial stability and empowerment—not by scarcity or shame. Together, let's begin rewriting your money story with intention, compassion, and unshakable determination.

## 6.2 Escaping the Paycheck-to-Paycheck Trap

Living paycheck to paycheck isn't just a matter of financial inconvenience—it can rob you of mental bandwidth, limit your options, and anchor you in survival mode. When every hard-earned dollar is allocated before it even reaches your hands, it can feel impossible to save, invest, or simply breathe without the pressure of looming bills. This draining cycle often intensifies for individuals reentering society with limited job prospects, or those who've incurred significant medical or legal debts.

However, escaping this pattern is entirely feasible. It requires more than short-term hustle; it demands strategy, discipline, and a shift from reactive to proactive money management. In the sections below, we'll examine three actionable methods to stabilize your finances: employing the 50/30/20 budgeting rule, establishing an emergency fund, and increasing your income through strategic action. Together, these steps create financial breathing room and begin moving you from simple survival to meaningful wealth-building.

### The 50/30/20 Rule for Financial Stability

A lack of structure is a primary reason many remain trapped in paycheck-to-paycheck living. Without a clear plan, every payday feels like a frantic dance—covering rent, paying overdue bills, juggling family expenses, and trying to carve out something for the future. The 50/30/20 rule, popularized by financial expert Elizabeth Warren, offers a straightforward approach to regaining balance:

1. **50% Needs** – Essentials like rent, utilities, groceries, insurance, and minimum debt payments.

2. **30% Wants –** Non-essentials: dining out, streaming services, hobbies, entertainment.

3. **20% Savings & Debt Repayment** – Emergency fund, investments, or extra debt payments.

For those barely affording basic needs, even hitting the 50% target may seem out of reach. In that scenario, reducing fixed costs becomes the first priority—downsizing living arrangements, finding cheaper transportation, or renegotiating utilities. If the 30% allocated to "wants" seems too generous, shifting more funds toward savings can expedite your path out of financial fragility.

The true power of this method lies in allocating money proactively instead of watching it vanish. Rather than feeling like your paycheck slips away instantly, you designate an intentional role for each dollar. This clarity not only imposes discipline on spending but also redirects resources toward building a foundation that safeguards you against the unexpected—particularly critical if legal fees or court-ordered financial obligations remain part of your reality.

## Building an Emergency Fund

For individuals caught in the paycheck-to-paycheck grind, unplanned events— car breakdowns, sudden medical bills, a job loss—can snowball into full-blown crises. An emergency fund becomes more than a distant luxury; it is your financial lifeline.

Start small. Even $500 set aside can prevent you from sliding into debt when life surprises you. Over time, aim to accumulate at least one month of expenses in a dedicated savings account, gradually working up to three to six months' worth of essentials. The question then is: Where do these funds come from?

- **Tiny, consistent contributions** – Even $10 or $20 per paycheck, automatically transferred to a separate account, can build momentum.

- **Unexpected windfalls** – Tax refunds, work bonuses, or side-hustle income should go directly into the emergency fund first, rather than being spent impulsively.

- **Automation** – Set up a system where a portion of your paycheck goes directly into savings, reducing reliance on willpower.

Having this financial buffer changes everything. Instead of feeling like you must rely on high-interest credit cards or predatory loans when unforeseen expenses crop up, you can tap into an emergency reserve. This not only preserves your mental energy—particularly precious if you're juggling probation requirements, medical issues, or family obligations—but also shields you from the kind of debt spiral that can keep you stuck in survival mode.

## How to Increase Income Through Strategic Action

While trimming costs can stabilize finances in the short term, true financial mobility often depends on raising your income. Where reducing expenses has practical limits, there's no hard ceiling on earning potential.

### 1. Maximizing Earning Potential in Your Current Role

For many, the quickest route to higher income involves enhancing their position at their existing workplace. A Payscale study revealed that employees who regularly seek raises end up earning significantly more over a career than those who never negotiate. Yet countless individuals—especially those burdened by the fear that a criminal record or employment gap might hinder them—shy away from salary discussions altogether.

Key strategies for increasing pay without switching jobs:

- **Request a raise** – Gather industry pay data, document your achievements, and schedule a meeting with your supervisor. Demonstrate how you've added value to the company.

- **Aim for promotion** – Identify skill gaps, volunteer for leadership tasks, and demonstrate initiative. Being proactive positions you favorably when advancement arises.

- **Upgrade high-value skills** – Certifications, specialized training, or additional education all enhance your value to an employer. Even short workshops can yield a stronger bargaining position in salary discussions.

## 2. Creating Additional Income Streams

If your current job offers limited growth—or you desire more control over your financial destiny—cultivating multiple income streams can be transformative.

**Potential options** include:

- **Freelancing** – Platforms like Upwork or Fiverr let you monetize abilities such as writing, graphic design, translation, or consulting.

- **Online Business** – E-commerce ventures, affiliate marketing, and digital products can generate scalable, sometimes passive, income.

- **Monetizing a Hobby** – Skills like cooking, tutoring, photography, or personal training can be turned into profitable side gigs.

- **Real Estate & Investing** – While requiring time or capital to start, rentals or index-fund investing can substantially accelerate wealth building over the long run.

The crucial element is to act now, even if everything isn't perfect. Earning an extra few hundred dollars a month—whether through a small business, weekend freelancing, or renting a room—provides a cushion that helps break dependence on a single paycheck. For individuals balancing parole, school, or therapy, such supplemental income can relieve pressing financial pressure and pave a practical path toward growth.

# 6.3 Rewiring for Wealth and Success

Wealth isn't just the total in a checking account—it's a mindset. Two people could draw the same paycheck, yet one may forever feel stressed and strapped, while the other steadily advances toward financial stability. The key difference lies not in the raw dollars they earn but in how they view money. Overcoming systemic or personal barriers—like having to manage restitution payments, sudden legal fees, or family members relying on a single source of income—can make it feel as though resources are perpetually scarce. Yet perspective, strategy, and financial literacy can transform what seems unattainable into a structured path toward an abundant future.

From a young age, many are taught to see money as scarce or morally fraught, particularly those who grew up watching financial strain compound under the weight of bail, fines, or limited job opportunities post-incarceration. By contrast, individuals who effectively build wealth treat money as a dynamic tool—one that, when handled well, fosters independence and opens doors. Fortunately, this viewpoint isn't inherited at birth—it can be learned. Through understanding how wealthy people think differently about money, establishing systems that let your finances grow, and embracing continued financial learning, you can escape the constraints of a paycheck-to-paycheck cycle or cyclical debt, forging a future marked by security and possibility.

## Why Rich People Think Differently About Money

Early childhood messages—like "What am I, rich?" or "Rich people are greedy"—often echo into adulthood. These beliefs shape how you might approach earnings, spending, and the possibility of ever getting ahead. Financially successful individuals defy these scripts: instead of regarding money as merely something to earn and spend, they treat it as capital to invest and multiply.

One major mindset shift among the affluent is recognizing that money can work for them. Rather than simply exchanging hours for wages, they design income streams that keep generating returns—even when they aren't clocked in. By contrast, many wage earners put in extended hours and count on occasional raises, never stepping off that treadmill of labor-for-pay. This difference becomes especially stark for those reentering the job market after legal setbacks, as reliance on a single paycheck can feel precarious; studying or experimenting with alternative income opportunities can be life-changing.

Another fundamental difference is that wealthy people don't fear money—they master it. Where some may avoid reviewing their bank statements out of anxiety or an ingrained sense of hopelessness, financially adept individuals treat budgeting and financial check-ins as a continuous strategic tool. Budgeting isn't burdening—it's systematic resource optimization. For people juggling obligations like restitution fees, child support, or pending loan payments, adopting a similar approach fosters clarity and a sense of command over their finances.

Many self-made millionaires, including Warren Buffett and Mark Cuban, attribute their prosperity to financial acumen, risk mitigation, and extended timelines, rather than sheer luck. The underlying principle is straightforward: Instead of tirelessly working for money, figure out how to make money work for you. Whether you do so by learning about index fund investments, renting out a spare room, or creating a small online side business, the shift from purely reactive spending to active wealth-building can reverse years of perceived impossibility—no matter how modest the starting point.

## How to Make Money Work for You

Money, when used correctly, can be a wealth-building machine. Yet, most people never learn how to leverage their earnings—they simply work, spend, and repeat the cycle. The wealthy break this pattern by using money to create more money.

Here's how:

- **Invest Instead of Just Save**

    Keeping money in a basic savings account isn't enough. Inflation eats away at its value over time. Wealthy individuals invest in assets—stocks, real estate, businesses—that grow their money over time. Even small investments compound into significant gains.

- **Prioritize Passive Income Streams**

  Active income (salary) is limited by time. Passive income—money earned from investments, rental properties, dividends, or automated businesses—continues to flow even when you're not working. The more passive income you create, the less dependent you become on a paycheck.

- **Control Expenses and Avoid Lifestyle Inflation**

  Many people assume that earning more means having more, but that's not true if spending increases just as quickly. The rich avoid lifestyle inflation—the tendency to upgrade cars, homes, and luxuries every time income rises. Instead, they reinvest their money, allowing their wealth to grow before indulging in major purchases.

- **Leverage Other People's Money (OPM)**

  Contrary to what most believe, the wealthy often use borrowed money strategically. Real estate investors use loans to acquire properties that generate more income than the mortgage costs. Entrepreneurs use business credit to scale operations. It's not about debt—it's about leverage.

- **Master the Power of Compound Growth**

  Albert Einstein famously called compound interest "the eighth wonder of the world." The earlier you start investing, the more your money compounds. A person investing $500 a month starting at age 25 will have far more wealth by retirement than someone investing $1,000 a month starting at 40. Time is the greatest asset in wealth-building, but it's never too late to start.

When you stop thinking of money as something to spend and start seeing it as something to grow, you take control of your financial destiny.

## The Importance of Financial Literacy

One of the greatest divides between the wealthy and the struggling isn't just income—it's financial knowledge. A person can win the lottery and still go broke, while another can start with nothing and become a millionaire. The difference? Financial literacy.

Unfortunately, traditional education rarely teaches how to manage money, invest wisely, or build wealth. That's why self-education is critical. Those who commit to understanding personal finance, investing, and money management gain an edge that lasts a lifetime.

Here's how to build financial literacy:

- **Read Books by Financial Experts**

  Classics like *Rich Dad Poor Dad* by Robert Kiyosaki, *The Millionaire Next Door* by Thomas Stanley, and *The Psychology of Money* by Morgan Housel offer game-changing insights into wealth-building.

- **Learn the Basics of Investing**

  Understanding how stocks, real estate, and retirement accounts work prevents financial mistakes and accelerates wealth growth. Platforms like Vanguard and Fidelity offer beginner-friendly resources.

- **Study How the Wealthy Manage Money**

  Research how successful people invest, budget, and leverage assets. The patterns are clear—wealth isn't built by accident, but by intentional financial strategy.

- **Take Control of Your Financial Data**

  Know your net worth, track spending, and monitor your credit score. Ignorance isn't bliss when it comes to money—it's a liability.

Financial literacy isn't about knowing everything at once—it's about committing to lifelong learning. The more financially educated you become, the more power you gain over your future.

## Real-World Resilience: Dave Ramsey's Financial Comeback

In his late twenties, Dave Ramsey was living the American dream—or so it seemed. He built a million-dollar real estate portfolio and was enjoying wealth beyond anything he had imagined. But beneath the surface, his finances were dangerously fragile. When the banking system tightened lending policies, Dave found himself drowning in debt, forced into bankruptcy, and deeply ashamed. He felt trapped, his self-worth shattered, his confidence destroyed by failure.

Dave knew he had two choices: remain stuck in shame, or face the painful truth about the unhealthy money habits that led him there. He chose to break the cycle, completely changing his relationship with money. He built new beliefs, better habits, and healthier patterns of decision-making. Over time, not only did Dave rebuild his wealth, he transformed his experience into a powerful mission. Today, as a bestselling author and financial expert, he's helped millions reclaim their lives from debt and financial despair.

Dave Ramsey's story reminds us that no matter the depth of the cycle we're caught in, whether financial, emotional, or relational, breaking free is possible

## 6.4 Taking Control of Your Financial Future

True financial independence is not just about earning more money—it's about taking control of your financial trajectory. Far too many people live reactively, waiting for the next paycheck, hoping for a promotion, or assuming that security will come "someday." But wealth doesn't happen by accident. It happens when you decide to take charge, educate yourself, and put your money to work.

The good news? Financial control isn't reserved for the wealthy or privileged—it's a skill set anyone can develop, even those who are recovering from life-altering hardships. By understanding the power of investing early, leveraging passive vs. active income, and creating multiple streams of revenue, you shift from being a participant in your financial story to the author of it.

## The Power of Investing Early

Time is the most formidable asset in building wealth—more influential than talent or even income. If you contribute $200 a month beginning at age 25, assuming an 8% average annual return, you could accumulate over $500,000 by retirement. Wait until 35, and the same monthly investment yields just $245,000. Delay another decade to 45, and the total plunges to $100,000.

However, the true advantage of investing early isn't merely about amassing bigger balances. It's about enabling every dollar to perform the heavy lifting over time. Funds deployed sooner have decades to multiply—a benefit that can prove critical for those grappling with the aftermath of incarceration or starting from scratch mid-career. While age might feel like a roadblock, especially for people in their 40s or 50s eager to recalibrate their future, compounding ensures that even modest sums steadily grow, giving new beginnings a genuine chance to flourish.

Many hesitate because investing can seem complicated or risky, so they postpone action. But postponement is arguably the greatest financial misstep. The key is to begin right where you are, however small that starting point might feel. Channel your resources consistently—be it through index funds, real estate ventures, or dividend stocks—and watch as those contributions snowball into remarkable wealth over time. Studies on investor behavior show that regular, automatic investments outperform sporadic, reactive ones by a wide margin.

Whether you're in your early 20s, living paycheck to paycheck, or you've reached mid-life rebuilding after trauma, the principle stands: Begin now. Your future self—months, years, or decades down the line—will look back and be profoundly grateful.

## Passive Income vs. Active Income

Most people only understand active income—trading time for money. A salary, an hourly wage, or freelance work all require constant effort to sustain. If you don't show up, the money stops. This is how most of the world operates.

Wealthy individuals, however, think differently. They prioritize passive income—income that continues to flow even when they're not actively working. Investments, rental properties, royalties, and automated businesses create streams of income that don't rely on daily labor. This is what allows the rich to build financial freedom while others stay trapped in the work-money cycle.

The goal isn't to eliminate active income—it's to leverage it to create passive income. Imagine working a 9-to-5 job but funneling 20% of your salary into assets that generate income on their own. Over time, your money begins working for you, and eventually, your passive income can replace your active income altogether.

Think of active income as the fuel that starts the engine and passive income as the engine that keeps running—whether you're working, sleeping, or traveling the world.

## How to Create Multiple Streams of Income

Financial security is fragile if it rests on a single income source. A job can be lost. A business can fail. An industry can collapse. This is why wealthy individuals never rely on just one stream of income—they create multiple.

Here are some proven ways to build diverse income streams:

- **Invest in Dividend Stocks**

  Stocks that pay dividends provide passive income without selling shares. Companies like Coca-Cola and Johnson & Johnson have paid increasing dividends for decades, rewarding investors for holding long term.

- **Real Estate Rentals**

  Owning rental properties allows you to collect income while the property appreciates in value. Even one well-chosen property can generate steady monthly cash flow. You may even think about using your property as transitional housing for others who are getting back on their feet if you are in that position.

- **Side Businesses and Freelancing**

  Starting an online business, consulting, or freelancing adds another source of income without quitting your job. Many people build six-figure side businesses while still working full-time. These are opportunities that are available to people regardless of their background. There are always creative ways to create a business, product, or service where your background has no relevance and can work within the parameters of your parole or probation terms.

- **Royalties and Digital Products**

  Writing a book, licensing intellectual property, or selling online courses and e-books can generate income long after the initial work is done. Unlike active income, these assets continue to pay you indefinitely.

- **Automated Investments**

  Investing in peer-to-peer lending, REITs (real estate investment trusts), or automated ETF portfolios can create passive growth without requiring hands-on management.

The key isn't to chase every income stream—it's to strategically build and diversify. Start with one, master it, and then expand into others. Over time, these income streams layer on top of each other, creating a financial ecosystem that thrives regardless of economic conditions.

## Daily Affirmations for Financial Success

Affirmations are not just motivational phrases—they are a neurological reprogramming tool. Your brain forms beliefs through repetition, meaning that the more you tell yourself something, the more your subconscious accepts it as truth.

To incorporate financial affirmations into your daily routine:

- **Choose statements that feel powerful and believable.** Instead of "I am a millionaire" (which your brain might reject if you're struggling financially), try "I am becoming financially free every day."

- **Pair affirmations with action.** Saying "Money flows to me easily" is great, but backing it up with strategic investments makes it far more effective.

- **Engage multiple senses.** Write affirmations down, say them aloud, and visualize them in action. The stronger the emotional connection, the faster your mind integrates them.

Some examples of effective financial affirmations:

- "I make wise financial decisions that build my wealth."
- "I am worthy of financial abundance and security."
- "Every dollar I invest works for me and multiplies."
- "I attract opportunities that increase my income effortlessly."

Saying them isn't enough—you must believe and embody them. As you internalize these statements, you begin making subtle but powerful shifts in your behavior, steering yourself toward financial success with confidence and clarity.

## Your Personal Wealth-Building Strategy

Wealth-building isn't a one-size-fits-all process. While foundational principles apply to everyone—saving, investing, increasing income streams—your wealth strategy must align with your unique goals, risk tolerance, and financial vision.

To create a personalized wealth-building blueprint, ask yourself:

1.  **What is my wealth goal?** Is it financial freedom? Retiring early? Building a real estate portfolio? Your strategy should be tailored to what success looks like for you.

2.  **What's my primary wealth-building vehicle?** Stocks, real estate, business ownership? Each requires different skills, patience levels, and risk appetites. Choose what aligns with your strengths.

3.  **How will I increase my income?** Saving is important, but you can't save your way to wealth. The rich prioritize increasing income—whether through business, investing, or high-income skills.

4.  **What financial habits will I automate?** The wealthy don't rely on willpower—they use systems. Automate savings, investments, and bill payments to ensure consistent financial growth.

5.  **What will I do differently this year?** Change doesn't happen without new action. Identify at least one major financial move you will make in the next three months—then commit to it.

By crafting a strategy that is specific, measurable, and adaptable, you build a financial roadmap that is clear and executable. This is how wealth stops being a dream and becomes a reality.

## Chapter 6 Case Study: Curtis "Wall Street" Carroll

### Background:

Born in 1978 in Washington, D.C., Curtis Carroll relocated to East Oakland, California, during his youth. Growing up amidst the challenges of the crack epidemic, Carroll faced significant hardships, including illiteracy and homelessness. At the age of 17, in 1996, he was arrested for burglary and murder, leading to a sentence of 54 years to life in prison, but ultimately served nearly 27 years.

**Application of Principles:**

- **Financial Empowerment and Wealth Mindset:** Carroll's journey exemplifies the transformative power of financial literacy and a wealth-oriented mindset. His story underscores the importance of understanding and managing finances as a pathway to personal empowerment and societal contribution.

- **Overcoming Poverty Mindset:** By educating himself and others about financial markets, Carroll broke free from the constraints of a poverty mindset, demonstrating that financial education can serve as a tool for rehabilitation and personal growth.

- **Taking Control of Financial Future:** Through his self-education and subsequent teaching efforts, Carroll took proactive steps to secure his financial future and assist others in doing the same, highlighting the role of financial literacy in fostering independence and reducing recidivism.

**Outcome:**

Curtis "Wall Street" Carroll's transformation from an illiterate inmate to a financial educator has garnered significant recognition. His TED Talk, "How I learned to read—and trade stocks—in prison," has amassed over 4.2 million views, inspiring audiences worldwide. Carroll's story has been featured in prominent publications such as The Wall Street Journal, Forbes, and NPR, highlighting his unique journey and the impact of his work. After serving nearly 27 years, Carroll was released from prison on December 10, 2022. Since his release, he has founded FEEL Inc., a financial wellness company focused on teaching financial literacy and emotional awareness, furthering his mission to empower others through financial education.

## 6.5 Action Plan – Creating Your Wealth Blueprint

Building wealth isn't just about making money—it's about crafting a financial blueprint that supports long-term success. This action plan includes a 30-day money mindset challenge, daily affirmations for financial success, and a customized wealth-building strategy designed to keep you on track.

## Weekly Wealth Plan

1.  **Week 1:** Awareness & Reflection (30 minutes):

    *   Track every thought and emotion tied to money. Notice patterns. Do you feel guilt when you spend? Do you associate wealth with stress? Identifying these beliefs is the first step in shifting them.

    *   Reflect on how these beliefs have impacted your financial decisions.

2.  **Week 2:** Rewriting the Narrative (30 minutes):

    *   For every limiting belief you uncover, rewrite it into a new, empowering statement. Instead of "I'm bad with money," replace it with "I am learning how to master my finances."

    *   Practice these new affirmations daily to reinforce positive financial beliefs.

3.  **Week 3:** Daily Wealth Habits (15 minutes):

    *   Implement one small financial habit per day—this could be automating savings, researching investments, or negotiating a bill. Small actions compound over time.

    *   Celebrate each small victory along the way.

4.  **Week 4:** Future Financial Identity (30 minutes):

    *   Visualize your ideal financial future. Who do you need to become to achieve it? Act as that person now—whether it's through strategic investing, disciplined budgeting, or entrepreneurial thinking.

    *   Develop a plan to embody this identity consistently.

5.  **Daily Affirmations (5 minutes):**

- Use daily affirmations to reinforce positive financial beliefs. Examples include:

  - "I am capable of managing my finances effectively."

  - "I trust myself to make wise financial decisions."

  - Repeat these affirmations daily to shift your mindset towards abundance.

## Monthly Reflection and Adjustment

- **Assess Your Progress:** Take time to reflect on how far you've come. Identify areas where you've improved and where you still need to work.

- **Adjust Your Plan:** Based on your reflections, adjust your weekly habits to better align with your financial goals.

## Additional Strategies for Success

1. **Automate Your Finances:** Set up automatic savings and bill payments to reduce decision fatigue and ensure consistent financial progress.

2. **Educate Yourself:** Continuously learn about personal finance, investing, and wealth-building strategies to make informed decisions.

3. **Surround Yourself with Support:** Engage with people who support and encourage your financial goals. This could include joining a financial support group or finding a mentor.

4. **Celebrate Small Wins:** Acknowledge and celebrate each small financial victory along the way. This helps build confidence and reinforces positive behaviors.

By following this action plan, you'll begin to shift from financial survival to financial mastery, creating a wealth blueprint that supports your long-term success.

# Chapter 6 Summary: Financial Success and Wealth Mindset Transformation

Financial success isn't just about numbers—it's about mindset, strategy, and taking control of your future. In this chapter, you learned that wealth isn't something you wait for—it's something you build. By shifting from a scarcity mindset to an abundance mindset, you've begun the process of breaking free from financial struggle and creating long-term security.

You now understand that escaping the paycheck-to-paycheck trap isn't just about budgeting—it's about increasing income, leveraging money wisely, and making wealth-building decisions. The wealthy don't just work for money—they make money work for them. By applying financial literacy, strategic investing, and smart money management, you gain the power to create a future where financial stability is no longer a dream, but a reality.

But true wealth isn't just measured in dollars—it's measured in confidence, resilience, and the belief that you are in control of your life.

In Chapter 7, we'll take this transformation even further by developing unshakable confidence and charisma—because success isn't just about what you have, but how you carry yourself. You'll learn how to walk into any room with certainty, handle criticism without breaking, and build the presence of a leader. After all, financial freedom means nothing if you don't believe in your own power to claim it.

# Chapter 7

## Developing Unshakable Confidence and Charisma

*"Confidence is not 'they will like me.' Confidence is 'I'll be fine if they don't.'"*– Christina Grimmie

Have you ever met someone who walks into a room and effortlessly commands attention—not because they're loud or demanding, but because there's a quiet certainty about them? It seems like some people are born with this natural confidence, while others struggle every day to feel like they're enough.

But here's the powerful truth: Confidence is not a trait you either have or you don't. It's a skill, a state of mind that you can learn, practice, and master. No matter what you've been through—whether it's trauma, incarceration, financial hardship, or personal loss—you can cultivate the kind of genuine, unshakable confidence that changes how you show up in every area of your life.

In this chapter, you'll discover the keys to building authentic confidence from the inside out. You'll learn how to overcome fear of rejection and criticism, carry yourself with charisma, and become someone who truly owns every room you walk into—not because you've become someone else, but because you've finally tapped into the extraordinary person you were always meant to be.

### Preview – Meet Reginald Dwayne Betts

At 16, Reginald Dwayne Betts stood before a judge who sentenced him to nearly a decade behind bars for a violent crime. He had every reason to lose faith in himself and his future. Yet, behind prison walls, Dwayne cultivated profound confidence and charisma through poetry and education. His journey from convicted felon to acclaimed poet, Yale-educated lawyer, and advocate illustrates the transformative power of confidence, even in the darkest moments.

You'll find Dwayne's remarkable story at the chapter's conclusion, including how he developed confidence and charisma from behind bars.

# 7.1 The Psychology of Confidence

Confidence isn't a mystical trait reserved for the fortunate few—it's a teachable skill built through deliberate effort, ongoing practice, and mindset shifts. Many assume confidence is something you either have or lack, but that perspective can be limiting. Instead, think of confidence as an ability shaped by action, repetition, and a willingness to embrace discomfort.

For individuals who've had interactions with the criminal justice system or facing adversity after a devastating personal loss, they may feel unsure, early on, weighed down by stigma or self-doubt. Yet each step—like learning a new skill, initiating important conversations, or simply trusting themselves to handle new challenges—strengthens the neural pathways in the brain responsible for resilience and self-assurance. As Dr. Carol Dweck explains with her concept of the growth mindset, people who treat challenges as opportunities to learn, push through setbacks, and view effort as a vehicle for mastery naturally cultivate a deeper sense of confidence.

Real transformation isn't about waiting until you "feel" confident; it's about acting as though you are confident, even when doubt lingers. Ask: *What would a more assured version of me do in this situation?* Adopting that line of thinking bridges the gap between where you stand now and the self-possessed individual you're striving to become.

### The "Fake It Until You Make It" Myth – And What to Do Instead

The idea of "fake it until you make it" can be tempting, but it's frequently misunderstood. While acting confident can provide a short burst of courage, authentic confidence grows from tangible successes and skills—particularly critical if you're navigating mid-life transitions or working to prove your reliability in a new environment.

If you rely solely on pretense, you risk sliding into imposter syndrome, feeling like a fraud despite external achievements. Instead of faking confidence, reinforce it with real-life practice. For example, someone who's been away from the workforce might start by volunteering or taking on small projects to gather "wins" that confirm their capabilities. Each time you follow through on a difficult task—be it leading a team meeting, presenting in front of a skeptical audience, or finishing a training program—your brain logs evidence that you're capable, reducing the sway of self-doubt.

According to neuroscientific research on mirror neurons, the way you carry yourself can also influence your internal state. Standing tall, making steady eye contact, and using open body language all signal confidence to your brain. This dual approach—physical embodiment paired with consistent action—cultivates genuine self-belief rather than an empty performance. So, while quick fixes might help you power through an immediate hurdle, it's the long-term ritual of facing challenges head-on that solidifies confidence for a lifetime.

Ultimately, confidence is an earned state, not a fleeting show. If you're learning how to trust your abilities again halfway through life, the surest path is practical, hands-on practice. By taking on real challenges, you steadily gather the evidence your mind needs to evolve from doubt into unwavering self-assurance.

## Reprogramming Self-Doubt into Self-Assurance

Self-doubt is the silent killer of confidence, and everyone struggles with it at some point in life, especially if you are in recovering from traumatic experiences. It's that nagging voice in your head that tells you you're not good enough, not smart enough, not capable enough. The problem isn't that the voice exists—it's that most people believe it.

The first step in reprogramming self-doubt is identifying and challenging negative self-talk. Pay attention to the internal dialogue running in your mind.

When you catch yourself thinking, *I'll embarrass myself* or *I'm not qualified for this*, ask yourself: Where's the evidence? More often than not, self-doubt is a conditioned response, not a fact.

One of the most effective ways to rewire your confidence is through affirmations, visualization, and mental rehearsal. Studies in cognitive psychology reveal that repeated exposure to positive affirmations strengthens neural pathways in the brain, making confidence more automatic over time. Instead of repeating generic phrases like *I am confident*, use specific affirmations that reinforce action:

- "I am prepared, and I trust myself to handle any challenge."
- "I bring value to every conversation I enter."
- "I am becoming more confident with every action I take."

Pairing affirmations with visualization amplifies their effect. Spend a few minutes each day mentally rehearsing the version of yourself who moves through life with certainty, no matter what you have endured. See yourself walking into a room, shoulders back, head high, speaking with authority and ease. Your brain doesn't distinguish between real and imagined experiences, so this practice conditions you to feel comfortable in situations before you even step into them.

Finally, develop a confidence trigger—a simple, repeatable action that shifts your mindset instantly. This could be a power pose, a deep breath, a certain song that energizes you, or a mantra you say before a big moment. The key is repetition. The more often you pair this action with a confident state, the more automatic the association becomes.

## 7.2  Body Language and Presence – Looking the Part

Confidence isn't just a mindset; it's a physical presence that communicates who you are and how you feel about yourself. Before you ever say a word, your body has already spoken for you. Whether in a job interview, social setting, or high-stakes negotiation, the way you carry yourself shapes how others perceive you. Research shows that people form judgments about confidence, competence, and trustworthiness within seconds. These snap evaluations, often subconscious, dictate whether people see you as a leader, a peer, or someone to overlook. The good news? You can control the message you send.

## The Science of First Impressions

The moment you walk into a room, your posture, facial expressions, and energy communicate your confidence and authenticity. According to a Princeton University study, it takes less than a second for people to form an impression based on your body language. Confidence is not just about appearing powerful; it's about control and authenticity. If your shoulders slump, your arms cross defensively, or your eyes dart around the room, you send signals of insecurity. Conversely, standing tall, maintaining steady eye contact, and holding an open posture instantly make you appear more competent and self-assured.

## Mastering Power Body Language

Your posture doesn't just change how others see you—it directly impacts how you feel about yourself. Harvard researcher Amy Cuddy found that adopting "power poses"—expansive, open body positions—can increase confidence and reduce stress. Techniques like the "Superman Pose" can be particularly effective: standing tall with your feet shoulder-width apart, hands on your hips, and head held high. Holding this stance for just two minutes has been shown to lower cortisol and boost testosterone, priming you for high-pressure situations.

Beyond power poses, your movements communicate authority. Confident people move with deliberate, controlled, and purposeful motions. Whether you're walking into a meeting, taking a seat, or gesturing during a conversation, slow, intentional movements project a sense of control. When you move with certainty, you exude an unspoken message: I belong here.

## Personal Reflection and Growth

After my arrest, I struggled to look anyone in the eye. The fear of being recognized left me feeling small and ashamed. It took me years to understand that I didn't have a flashing neon "offender" sign over my head. It was my own perception that made me feel like I didn't belong. Eventually, I found ways to laugh again, be my true self, and embody confidence through my body language. This transformation wasn't just about others' perceptions; it was about reclaiming my own sense of self-worth. Most people I meet now would never know by looking at me that I've been on probation, rebuilding my life after an arrest. As I learned to rebuild my confidence, I realized that small actions like maintaining eye contact could significantly impact how others perceive me.

## Using Your Voice to Exude Confidence

Your voice is one of the most powerful tools you have. It's not just what you say—it's how you say it. Studies have shown that people with a calm, controlled, and deliberate tone are perceived as more authoritative. If your voice shakes, trails off, or rises at the end of every sentence, it signals doubt. But when your voice is steady, your pace measured, and your words deliberate, you command attention effortlessly.

### Practical Exercises for Vocal Confidence

To refine your vocal confidence, try these exercises:

1. **Record Yourself:** Record yourself speaking about a topic for one minute. Listen carefully to your tonality, speed, and inflection. Identify areas for improvement.

2. **Practice Lower Register:** Speak in a lower register (but not forced) to project authority.

3. **Breathe Deeply:** Breathe deeply before speaking—short, shallow breaths create nervous-sounding speech.

4. **Read Aloud Daily:** Read aloud for five minutes daily, deliberately focusing on pace, clarity, and projection.

Your voice is an extension of your presence. When you control it, you shape the way others perceive your confidence and credibility.

# 7.3  Social Confidence – Owning Any Room You Walk Into

Social confidence isn't about being the most outgoing or naturally extroverted person in the crowd—it's about feeling secure enough to engage with others without that gnawing sense of self-doubt. Whether you step into a professional networking session, a community support group, or a gathering of friends, your level of confidence shapes how others perceive you and how effectively you connect.

For individuals rebuilding after incarceration, grappling with stigma, or facing the complexities of financial or emotional upheaval, social anxiety can become an unseen barrier that keeps them in the background. It may appear as overthinking every exchange, bracing for others' judgment, or freezing when confronted with small talk. The reality is that social confidence isn't an inborn gift—it's a skill that can grow stronger with strategic practice.

## Understanding the Root of Social Fear and How to Dismantle It

At its core, social anxiety often centers on the dread of negative evaluation— what psychologists call the "spotlight effect", the misguided belief that everyone else is continuously scrutinizing your every word and gesture. In truth, most people are too immersed in their own thoughts to fixate on your every move. Researchers like Dr. David Moscovitch highlight that social anxiety feeds on these distorted perceptions, making events like job interviews or community gatherings feel like proving grounds for your worth.

This heightened self-consciousness frequently harks back to early experiences— perhaps an embarrassing mishap in front of peers, or growing up in an environment that didn't encourage speaking up. However, the past needn't define the future. Recognizing that fear is typically more perception than fact is crucial. Studies show that cognitive reframing—actively challenging negative assumptions—can shift your body's fear response. For instance, replacing thoughts like *"They'll think I'm awkward"* with *"People here are just as nervous as I am"* softens anxiety and opens the door to calmer, more genuine interaction.

## Exposure Therapy: The Step-by-Step Approach to Feeling Comfortable in Social Settings

True confidence is forged through action rather than avoidance. One effective technique for tackling social fear is exposure therapy, involving gradual, measured experiences in settings that gently push your boundaries without overwhelming you.

- **Start with Small, Manageable Interactions**

  If initiating conversation feels impossible, begin with simpler steps— perhaps greeting the cashier at the store, or complimenting someone's outfit. Each minor success becomes a "win" for your brain, diminishing its threat response and enhancing self-assurance.

- **Build Momentum, Increase Challenge**

  After you're at ease with small talk, escalate the complexity. Attend a small potluck or talk with a few new coworkers at once. Consistency, rather than sporadic effort, underpins growth. The more your mind experiences socializing without catastrophe, the weaker your anxiety's hold becomes.

- **Cultivate Curiosity, Not Performance**

  Shifting your attention from yourself to the person you're speaking with can reduce internal pressure. Show genuine interest—ask open-ended questions and listen intently. Research in social neuroscience indicates that focusing on another's perspective can lower self-conscious rumination, especially if you're concerned about legal or social stigma you can't hide. By actively listening, you transform anxiety into authentic connection.

### The "Inner Circle" Confidence Trick—How to Start Small and Expand Outward

A helpful tactic for navigating big social events is the Inner Circle Confidence Trick. Rather than thrusting yourself into every conversation, anchor your energy in a smaller, safer social nucleus and grow outward from there.

Picture entering a bustling room—maybe it's a reentry support group you're new to, or a large family event after an extended absence. Instead of tackling multiple people at once, approach one approachable person or a small circle. Once you strike up a rapport—whether it's sharing a bit about your day-to-day challenges or discussing a recent triumph in your job search—you begin to relax. That sense of comfort spreads to the rest of your interactions.

As your assurance climbs, lean on these fledgling connections to bridge into wider circles. When you've been speaking with someone for a bit, invite others into the conversation. Let introductions develop organically, and soon you'll be engaging with multiple people, feeling less forced and more at ease.

This method works because it grants your brain a window to acclimate before intensifying the social stakes. Gradually, you'll see that confidence isn't a fixed trait you either have or lack; it's something that develops moment by moment, chat by chat, especially in challenging settings like reentry job fairs, new workplaces, or larger community gatherings. Before long, you'll find yourself speaking up or leading conversations in rooms you used to avoid, discovering the deep satisfaction that comes with owning any room you walk into.

## 7.4 Overcoming Rejection and Criticism with Resilience

Rejection and criticism—two terms that evoke discomfort yet remain vital milestones on the path toward transformation. Anyone striving to rebuild after incarceration, loss, or a major crisis will inevitably face rejection; anyone bold enough to stand out will experience criticism. The divide between those who press forward and those who retreat often comes down to how they interpret these challenges instead of letting them dictate their self-worth.

It's crucial to see rejection not as a verdict on your character, nor criticism as a precise gauge of your capabilities. Both serve as external feedback—clues you can use to refine, grow, and adapt. Far too frequently, people allow such experiences to unravel their confidence, leaving them hesitant and afraid to attempt anything new. The pages ahead explore techniques and mindsets to help you transform rejection into forward momentum, convert criticism into a catalyst for improvement, and ensure that outside opinions no longer steer your sense of value.

## Real-World Resilience: Amanda Knox's Path to Confidence After Public Shaming

At 20 years old, Amanda Knox was living abroad as a college student in Italy when her life became a nightmare. Wrongfully accused and convicted of murdering her roommate, Amanda was subjected to relentless global scrutiny and brutal character assassination by international media. Headlines twisted her identity, portraying her as someone she didn't recognize, destroying her confidence and reputation.

After four agonizing years in an Italian prison, Amanda was finally exonerated, but the damage to her reputation and confidence seemed irreversible. Instead of hiding away in shame, Amanda made a courageous choice. She openly confronted the distorted narratives about her, reclaiming her story, rebuilding her self-confidence, and stepping back into the spotlight as an advocate against wrongful convictions.

Today, Amanda Knox uses her experiences to teach others the importance of finding your voice, embracing your true identity, and developing unshakable confidence—no matter how fiercely others might try to tear you down.

## Why Rejection is a Part of Success

Every Successful Person Has Faced Rejection—It's Not Personal, It's Just Redirection. Rejection isn't a proof of incompetence; it's a signpost indicating you may need to pivot. Notable high achievers throughout history encountered severe setbacks that would have led many to quit. Walt Disney lost his job at a newspaper for "lack of imagination." Oprah Winfrey was deemed unsuitable for television. These are not exceptions but the common thread among individuals who dare to achieve big. Rejection isn't personal—*it's data telling you, perhaps not now, not yet, or not in this way.* Your role is to resist internalizing it as a personal shortcoming and instead ask: *What lessons can I draw from this experience? Is there a different route I should explore?*

## How to Separate Your Self-Worth from External Validation

One of the most damaging traps is tying external acceptance to internal worth. When you get a "yes," you feel validated; when you get a "no," you feel diminished. This pattern is especially precarious if you've been turned down repeatedly for jobs due to a criminal record or have faced stigma for your past. However, true confidence stems from recognizing that you remain inherently valuable, regardless of someone else's verdict.

While it stings not to land the job, secure the apartment, or get a date, it simply means this particular route or timing wasn't right. Your core worth, shaped by your willingness to learn and change, stands untouched. As Dr. Angela Duckworth notes, resilience is not just about bouncing back from setbacks but also about learning from them. This mindset allows us to view rejections or failures as opportunities for growth rather than reflections of our worth. By embracing this perspective, we can maintain our core self-worth even when faced with external challenges.

## The "Rejection Reframing" Technique—Turning Failure into Fuel

Instead of labeling rejection as a crisis, treat it like a teacher. Assess each "no" or "not yet" by asking:

- **What specific feedback (if any) was provided?**

- **Could this opportunity have truly served my aspirations, or is a better one on the horizon?**

- **How can I alter my approach, refine my skills, or shift my strategy?**

Rejection doesn't command the final word on your life trajectory—it offers knowledge. Adopting this perspective reclaims your personal power, changing every "no" into a stepping-stone toward a future "yes." For those restarting mid-life, embracing that viewpoint is transformative. The more you view rejection as a form of redirection or new instruction, the more unstoppable your progress becomes.

## Handling Criticism Without Losing Confidence

Not all criticism is created equal. Some feedback is genuinely valuable—it offers insight that helps you improve. Other criticism is nothing more than someone else's insecurity masquerading as advice. The key is learning to separate the two.

- **Constructive criticism** comes from people who want to see you succeed. It's specific, actionable, and well-intentioned. Example: "Your presentation was strong, but working on your delivery speed could make it even more impactful."

- **Destructive criticism** is vague, personal, and demotivating. It doesn't offer solutions—it just tears down. Example: "That was terrible. You should probably quit."

When receiving criticism, ask yourself: Is this coming from someone whose opinion I respect? Is this feedback actionable, or is it just negativity? Learning to filter criticism keeps you from internalizing words that were never meant to help you.

## The "Mental Shield" Method to Protect Your Confidence

Imagine an invisible shield around you—one that absorbs useful criticism and deflects unnecessary negativity. When criticism comes your way, pause and mentally ask:

1. **Is this feedback useful?** If yes, integrate it and grow.

2. **Is this just someone else projecting their insecurities?** If so, let it bounce off your shield.

3. **Does this affect my long-term goals?** If not, move forward without a second thought.

The greatest performers, leaders, and innovators all developed mental resilience against criticism. They knew that if they let every opinion shape them, they'd lose themselves entirely.

## Why Most Critics Are Projecting Their Own Insecurities

Criticism often says more about the critic than the person being criticized. Many people tear others down to make themselves feel bigger. They project their own fears and limitations onto those who dare to step up.

Think of every troll on the internet, every toxic coworker, every person who sneers at someone genuinely rebuilding their life and reinventing themselves. They are not reflecting reality—they are exposing their own internal struggles. Once you realize this, their words lose power over you.

## How to Stop Caring What Others Think

## Understanding Why People's Opinions Have Less Power Than You Think

One of the greatest mental shifts you can make is realizing this truth: Most people aren't thinking about you as much as you think they are.

Psychologists call this the "spotlight effect"—the tendency to believe we're being observed and judged more than we actually are. But in reality, most people are too wrapped up in their own thoughts, insecurities, and problems to spend much time analyzing your actions.

Realizing this is liberating. It means you don't need to overanalyze every interaction, every social media post, or every choice you make. The opinions of others are just passing thoughts, not universal truths.

**The 3-Step Mental Exercise to Detach from External Validation**
When you feel consumed by what others think, try this:

1. **Ask yourself: Will this matter in five years?** Most things we stress over are temporary. If it won't matter long-term, don't let it consume you now.

2. **Reframe judgment as irrelevance.** If someone criticizes you, ask: Would I trade lives with them? If not, why give their opinion power over yours?

3. **Redirect focus inward.** Instead of seeking validation externally, validate yourself. If you know your worth, outside opinions become irrelevant.

## Developing Inner Confidence That Isn't Affected by Outside Judgment

Real confidence is rooted in self-trust. When you know who you are, what you stand for, and what you're working toward, external noise becomes just that—noise. The key is focusing on progress, not approval. Keep learning, growing, and pushing forward. As you build momentum in your personal and professional life, confidence becomes a natural byproduct.

## My Journey with Inner Confidence

Real confidence is rooted in self-trust—the unshakable belief that your worth isn't determined by external validation. When you know who you are, what you stand for, and what you're working toward, the judgments of others become background noise. Yet, this kind of inner confidence doesn't come easily, especially when rebuilding your life after trauma, systemic barriers, or personal loss.

Throughout my probation experience, I faced the daunting challenge of stepping into courtrooms to request modifications and permissions. Each time, I encountered new judges and state attorneys who didn't know me beyond the limited scope of my file. Despite the progress I had made in therapy to recover from guilt and shame and rebuild my life, these interactions were soul-crushing. The professionals who worked with me daily—advocating for my growth— were often dismissed, and my detailed evaluation reports rarely received more than a cursory glance.

At first, I approached these situations as though I was asking for permission to exist entirely, rather than requesting temporary conditional freedoms. Even when some requests were approved, celebrating felt hollow because I felt misunderstood and dismissed as a human being. Over time, however, I came to understand that these individuals were simply fulfilling their roles within a system designed to prioritize procedure over personal nuance. It wasn't their job to truly know me or understand the complexities of my story.

## Reclaiming My Narrative

I realized that my personal narrative would never truly be given space in that courtroom; in that context, I would always be seen through the lens of my charges rather than my humanity. But this limitation was theirs—not mine. Slowly but surely, I began to detach from their judgments and focus on the truth of who I was becoming outside those walls. Each time I entered the room, I carried with me a growing sense of self-worth—not because of their decisions but because of the work I was doing to rebuild my life.

I learned to take the victories with gratitude and approach the denials with patience, knowing that opportunities would arise again with new judges or circumstances. Most importantly, I stopped accepting their value judgments as definitive statements about my humanity. That power belonged to me alone.

This shift wasn't just about surviving those courtroom experiences—it was about reclaiming my right to exist fully and unapologetically. I deserve to take up space, move beyond my worst moment, and pursue happiness…just as my former student deserves her own path toward healing and growth, being allowed to move beyond the label and role of victim. Self-worth isn't something anyone can give or take away; it's something we must cultivate within ourselves despite the labels the world gives us.

## Finding Strength in Self-Validation

As I continued to face these challenges, my ability to bounce back from what I perceived as personal judgments grew stronger. I learned to focus on the victories and be patient with the denials, knowing that opportunities would arise again with new judges and circumstances. Most importantly, I understood that I couldn't accept others' value judgments on my humanity. That was for me alone to decide.

This journey taught me that true confidence isn't about external validation; it's about trusting yourself and your journey. By focusing on your growth and progress, you can build a sense of self-worth that isn't shaken by external opinions.

# Chapter 7 Case Study: Reginald Dwayne Betts

## Background:

Reginald Dwayne Betts was born in Maryland and displayed academic promise from a young age, participating in gifted programs and serving as class treasurer at Suitland High School in District Heights, Maryland. However, at the age of 16, Betts made a life-altering decision that led to his involvement in an armed carjacking at the Springfield Mall in Virginia. Tried as an adult, he was sentenced to nine years in prison, during which he spent over eight years incarcerated, including fourteen months in solitary confinement.

## Application of Principles:

- **Embracing a Growth Mindset:** While incarcerated, Betts confronted the consequences of his actions and sought personal development. He immersed himself in literature and poetry, transforming his cell into a space of learning and reflection. This shift in mindset allowed him to envision a future beyond the prison walls.

- **Cultivating Resilience:** Enduring the challenges of incarceration, including extended periods in solitary confinement, Betts developed resilience. He used writing as a coping mechanism, channeling his experiences into poetry that articulated the struggles and hopes of those incarcerated.

- **Pursuing Education and Skill Development:** Betts's commitment to self-improvement led him to complete his high school education while in prison. After his release, he continued his academic journey, earning a Bachelor of Arts from the University of Maryland, an MFA from Warren Wilson College, and a Juris Doctor from Yale Law School.

## Notable Achievements:

- **Literary Contributions:** Betts has authored three acclaimed poetry collections—*Shahid Reads His Own Palm (2010), Bastards of the Reagan Era (2015),* and *Felon (2019). His memoir, A Question of Freedom: A Memoir of Learning, Survival, and Coming of Age in Prison (2009),* received the 2010 NAACP Image Award for Outstanding Literary Work.

- **Advocacy and Legal Work:** Appointed by President Barack Obama in 2012, Betts served on the Coordinating Council of the Office of Juvenile Justice and Delinquency Prevention. He founded Freedom Reads, a nonprofit organization dedicated to providing incarcerated individuals with access to literature, fostering a love for reading and personal growth.

- **Academic and Professional Roles:** Betts is an Associate Research Scholar in Law at Yale Law School and a Visiting Lecturer on English at Harvard University, where he educates and inspires future leaders on topics intersecting law, literature, and social justice.

- **Awards and Honors:** His contributions have been recognized with several prestigious awards, including a 2018 Guggenheim Fellowship and a 2021 MacArthur Fellowship, often referred to as the "Genius Grant."

## Outcome:

Reginald Dwayne Betts's transformation from a teenager convicted of a serious crime to a distinguished poet and legal advocate exemplifies the profound impact of personal growth, education, and resilience. His journey underscores the potential for redemption and the importance of providing opportunities for self-improvement, even within the confines of incarceration. Through his literary works and advocacy, Betts continues to influence discussions on criminal justice reform and the power of literature to effect change.

## 7.5 Action Plan – Daily Confidence-Building Exercises

Confidence isn't a switch you flip—it's a muscle you build. And like any muscle, it strengthens with repetition, deliberate action, and progressive challenge. This action plan provides a structured approach to embedding confidence into your daily life, ensuring that self-assurance and presence become second nature.

### Weekly Confidence Plan

1. **Week 1: Building Foundations (30 minutes):**
   - Engage in the "Daily Confidence Challenge" by completing small, confidence-building tasks each day. For example:
     - **Day 1:** Make eye contact and smile at five strangers.
     - **Day 5:** Speak up in a group conversation.
   - Reflect on how these small actions make you feel more confident.

2. **Week 2: Expanding Your Comfort Zone (30 minutes):**

   - Gradually push your comfort zone by taking on slightly more challenging tasks. For instance:

     - **Day 9:** Compliment someone without hesitation.

     - **Day 14:** Share a personal opinion in a group setting.

   - Use daily self-reflection prompts to track your progress:

     - What small moment today made me feel more confident?

     - What challenge pushed me outside my comfort zone?

3. **Week 3:** Mindset and Visualization (15 minutes):

   - **Practice morning affirmations to prime your mind for confidence. Examples include:**

     - "I am confident in my abilities and trust myself in every situation."

     - "I speak with clarity, conviction, and purpose."

   - Spend two minutes visualizing yourself as the most confident version of yourself. Imagine walking into a room with effortless confidence and engaging with ease.

4. **Week 4:** Physical Confidence and Accountability (30 minutes):

   - Start each day with a 5-minute body language and voice warm-up:

     - Stand tall, chest open, shoulders relaxed.

     - Take deep, diaphragmatic breaths.

     - Do a voice warm-up by humming, stretching your vocal range, and practicing deliberate articulation.

   - Find a confidence accountability partner and check in weekly to discuss wins, challenges, and next steps.

5. **Daily Reflection and Celebration (5 minutes):**

- Keep a "Confidence Log" to document every moment where you stepped outside your comfort zone.

- Celebrate small victories daily, acknowledging each time you feel more confident.

### Monthly Reflection and Adjustment

- **Assess Your Progress:** Take time to reflect on how far you've come. Identify areas where you've improved and where you still need to work.

- **Adjust Your Plan:** Based on your reflections, adjust your weekly habits to better align with your confidence goals.

### Additional Strategies for Success

1. **Consistency is Key:** Make confidence-building exercises a daily habit to see consistent growth.

2. **Seek Feedback:** Ask your accountability partner for feedback on areas where you can improve.

3. **Celebrate Progress:** Acknowledge and celebrate each small victory along the way. This helps build confidence and reinforces positive behaviors.

By following this action plan, you'll begin to build confidence as a natural part of who you are, transforming the way you see yourself and how you show up in the world.

## Chapter 7 Summary: Developing Unshakable Confidence and Charisma

Confidence isn't something you're born with—it's something you build, refine, and strengthen through consistent effort and self-awareness. In this chapter, you uncovered how confidence is not about eliminating doubt, but about refusing to let it control you. You learned how to reshape your self-talk, master body language, and develop a presence that commands respect.

Beyond internal self-assurance, you explored social confidence—the ability to walk into any room with certainty, to own your space, and to handle interactions without fear. Through deliberate exposure and strategic practice, you've begun to break free from the anxiety that once held you back.

But confidence isn't just about showing up—it's about how you respond when things don't go your way. The most self-assured people aren't immune to rejection or criticism—they've simply learned to see them as redirections rather than roadblocks. You now have the tools to filter constructive feedback from negativity, detach self-worth from external opinions, and use setbacks as stepping stones toward greater success.

Yet confidence alone isn't enough—sustaining success requires turning these new habits into an unshakable identity.

In Chapter 8, we'll take everything you've learned so far and lock in your transformation, ensuring that your progress doesn't fade with time. You'll discover how to make success automatic, so discipline, resilience, and confidence become second nature—allowing you to sustain your growth without constantly forcing yourself to stay on track.

# Chapter 8

# Making Success Automatic – How to Sustain Your Transformation

*"We are what we repeatedly do. Excellence, then, is not an act, but a habit." –* Will Durant

A personal breakthrough can feel electrifying—like stumbling upon a hidden reservoir of strength you never knew existed. Yet the real challenge emerges after that initial burst of determination fades. Why do people who appear on the cusp of lasting change so often find themselves returning to past habits? The answer lies in our innate pull toward what's familiar, the comfort of old routines, and an underlying reluctance to embrace the new. Success isn't just reaching a better place; it's learning how to stay there, making progress feel like a permanent shift rather than a fleeting phase. In this chapter, you'll discover how to create lasting change through simple, repeatable habits, ensuring your success becomes automatic, sustainable, and deeply ingrained in your everyday life.

## Preview – Meet Dr. Stanley Andrisse

Stanley Andrisse was told by a judge that he would be a menace to society, forever defined by his criminal convictions and incarcerations. Stanley refused to accept this fate. Instead, he transformed his life through structured, identity-based habits and an unwavering belief in his potential. Today, Dr. Andrisse is not only an accomplished scientist and professor, but a mentor guiding countless others from prison cells to PhDs. His story reveals the incredible power of automating success through disciplined habits and routines.

Stanley's complete path to success is revealed at the end of this chapter, illustrating how habits turned him into a powerful example of resilience.

## 8.1 Why Most People Fall Back into Old Patterns

For individuals rebuilding after incarceration, financial devastation, or profound personal loss, this problem intensifies. Motivational surges can transform how you approach job interviews, personal relationships, or mental health, yet the lure of past routines runs deep. Psychologists explain that the mind naturally seeks homeostasis—returning to what's been normal for so long. Whether it's sliding back into a quick-fix mindset or avoiding the pursuit of new opportunities, the subconscious often calls you to revert.

True success involves embracing growth as the norm. Instead of viewing improvement as an event, treat it like a lifestyle. High achievers in any field rarely "settle"; once they've adapted to a new level of confidence, skill, or sobriety, they aim for the next horizon. To them, discomfort isn't a red flag but a sign of expanding potential. Studies confirm that consistent engagement in challenging tasks fosters the mental resilience needed to break old patterns and maintain upward momentum.

### The Comfort Zone Trap

The human brain is wired to conserve energy, preferring routine to innovation. Familiar habits—no matter how unproductive—offer predictability and security. This can be especially strong if you've spent years living in a cycle of negative self-talk or abiding by limiting external labels, such as "ex-offender" or "inadequate." Once real progress begins, your subconscious may start nudging you back to the old ways, whispering, *This is too risky* or *You don't really belong here.*

Imagine someone who, after decades of self-doubt, has finally begun to find their voice—perhaps speaking at local reentry events or applying for roles they once thought out of reach. Then that primal sense of "this feels unsafe" creeps in, urging them to keep quiet or stay in the background. This phenomenon echoes what psychologists describe as the "upper-limit problem," where any substantial positive change triggers anxiety about losing your familiar identity.

The route around this is making discomfort your friend. Each time you lean into an unfamiliar challenge—be it finishing a certification program, networking with professionals, or sharing your story publicly—you widen your comfort zone. Over time, new behaviors become standard, and "homeostasis" redefines itself around progress, not stagnation.

## How to Prevent Self-Sabotage Before It Starts

One of the most perplexing ironies of success is self-sabotage: just when you've gained real traction, the urge to shrink or derail sets in. Often, it isn't rooted in laziness or lack of ambition, but fear—fear of what success might demand, fear of the scrutiny that comes with stepping up, or fear of how relationships and responsibilities may shift.

This pattern manifests in countless forms:

- The entrepreneur who, after finally generating revenue, suddenly stops promoting their services.

- The individual who's maintained sobriety, then rationalizes a "small indulgence" that morphs into a full return to old addiction habits.

- The new hire, fresh out of prison or extended unemployment, who starts missing shifts the moment management begins to notice their potential.

These behaviors are rarely random. They emerge from a part of the psyche longing for the safety of the familiar. Researchers point out that, in high-stress transitions, your brain interprets rapid progress as a threat to equilibrium. Disrupting the cycle of self-sabotage involves anticipating triggers early. Ask yourself:

- *What emotional cues arise right before I relapse into old tendencies?*

- *Which justifications do I cling to when I edge away from my new path?*

- *What deeper discomfort am I hoping to bypass?*

By identifying these emotional markers, you can halt the backslide before it escalates. The goal isn't perfect adherence but an awareness that fosters quick course corrections. Real success evolves not from faultless execution but from repeated acts of noticing, adjusting, and recommitting.

## The Psychology of Long-Term Success

What truly separates those who sustain success from those who see it slip away? In essence, it's identity combined with systems. Identity is the linchpin. If you frame your achievements as something you're temporarily trying on— like "I'm attempting to be more disciplined"—then your brain can easily revert to "This isn't who I really am." But once you affirm, *I am disciplined*, you fuse your new behavior to your self-concept, and sustaining it demands less mental strain.

Additionally, lasting success thrives on gentle self-correction rather than harsh self-criticism. At times, the old habits will resurface—maybe you skip a week at the gym or slip on crucial job-search tasks. Instead of labeling these moments as a catastrophe, treat them as data that guide minimal adjustments. People who maintain success over the long haul don't interpret occasional missteps as proof of failure; they see them as signals to fine-tune.

If you're rebuilding your life, these systems and identity shifts matter profoundly. By weaving progress into your everyday routines and consistently reaffirming *This is who I am now*, you transition from temporary motivation to enduring transformation—proving that genuine change, once gained, can indeed become your new normal.

## Real-World Resilience: James Clear's Journey from Tragedy to Lasting Change

James Clear's life changed instantly during his sophomore year of high school, when a baseball bat struck him in the face during a game, fracturing his skull, shattering his identity as an athlete, and leaving him struggling physically and mentally. Doctors were uncertain whether he'd ever fully recover. James faced a long road of rehabilitation and was forced to redefine who he was and what his future would look like.

Yet James discovered something powerful in his struggle: the profound impact of small, consistent habits. Rather than accepting defeat, he chose a path of small, deliberate, daily actions, gradually rebuilding his body, mind, and confidence. His commitment to habits and routines didn't just restore his life—it transformed it. Today, James Clear is the bestselling author of "Atomic Habits," impacting millions by teaching the extraordinary power of incremental, sustainable change.

James' journey demonstrates clearly that making success automatic—sustaining your transformation over the long term—is entirely possible, no matter what setbacks you face.

## 8.2 The Power of Identity-Based Habits

Success is not just about setting goals and taking action—it's about becoming the kind of person for whom success is inevitable. Many people chase achievements by focusing on external behaviors, but true transformation happens when you internalize success as part of your identity. Instead of trying to "do" disciplined things, you must become a disciplined person. Instead of forcing yourself to act confident, you must see yourself as someone who embodies confidence. When success is integrated into your identity, the right habits follow effortlessly.

## Why Success Must Be WHO You Are, Not Just What You Do

Most people try to change their lives from the outside in. They set ambitious goals, implement strict routines, and push themselves through willpower alone. But external effort is exhausting without an internal shift. If deep down, you still see yourself as someone who struggles with discipline, finances, or confidence, you will always revert to old behaviors—because your actions will eventually align with your self-perception.

Think about the difference between these two statements:

- *"I need to work out more."* (Outcome-based thinking)
- *"I am someone who takes care of my body."* (Identity-based thinking)

The first approach makes exercise feel like a task, something separate from who you are. The second approach makes it a natural extension of your identity. When you embrace identity-based habits, success stops being a struggle—it becomes second nature.

## How to Build Effortless, Success-Driven Habits

Effortless success isn't about eliminating work—it's about eliminating resistance. When a habit feels forced, it's because it conflicts with your subconscious self-image. The solution? Redefine yourself in alignment with the habits you want to cultivate.

Start by asking yourself:

- Who is the kind of person that achieves the success I desire?
- What would that person do daily, effortlessly?
- How can I start embodying that today?

If you want to be financially successful, don't just try to *save money*—become the person who is *financially responsible*. If you want to be productive, *don't just force yourself to work*—see yourself as *someone who values focus and efficiency.*

One powerful method to reinforce identity-driven habits is visualization combined with immediate action. Neuroscientists have found that when you mentally rehearse a habit, your brain fires as if you were actually doing it, strengthening the neural pathways that support the behavior. This means that each time you act in alignment with your new identity, even in small ways, you make it easier to sustain long-term.

For example, if you decide to embody discipline, start small but act immediately. Wake up at a consistent time, make your bed, plan your day. These actions might seem insignificant, but they serve as daily reinforcements of your new identity. Success-driven habits become effortless when they no longer feel like a task but a reflection of who you are.

## Using Habit Stacking to Reinforce Your New Mindset

Building new habits can feel overwhelming—unless you attach them to routines you already have. This is where habit stacking, a concept popularized by behavioral scientists, becomes a game-changer.

Habit stacking works by anchoring a new habit to an existing one, making it easier to remember and execute. Instead of starting from scratch, you use the momentum of routines already in place.

Examples of habit stacking:

- After I brush my teeth, I will read one page of a book (to reinforce a learning habit).

- Before I check my phone in the morning, I will write down three things I'm grateful for (to cultivate a positive mindset).

- When I pour my morning coffee, I will say my top three affirmations out loud (to reinforce self-belief).

The key is pairing new habits with behaviors that are already automatic. By doing this, success habits integrate into your life seamlessly, without the mental strain of building them from scratch.

Habit stacking also creates compounding benefits—when small, positive actions are repeated consistently, they create exponential growth. Imagine how your life will look after stacking just three powerful habits each day. What seems like minor adjustments now can completely shift your identity and trajectory over time.

## 8.3 Your Personal Success Blueprint

A goal without a plan is just a wish. Success isn't built on wishful thinking—it's engineered with precision. If you want to create a life of achievement, and leave the past behind, you need a blueprint that turns your ambitions into structured, measurable progress. The most successful individuals don't leave their future to chance; they define it, break it down into actionable steps, and build systems that guarantee results.

This is where the Personal Success Blueprint comes in—a framework designed to help you create a compelling long-term vision, reverse-engineer it into daily actions, and construct a system that ensures continuous progress.

### Creating a Vision for the Next 5 Years

Where do you want to be five years from now? Most people drift through life, reacting to circumstances instead of designing their future. The problem isn't a lack of desire—it's a lack of clarity. Without a well-defined vision, you'll expend energy on distractions instead of meaningful progress.

Start by answering this question: *If everything in my life aligned perfectly, what would my ideal reality look like in five years?* Think about your career, finances, health, relationships, and personal growth. Be specific. The clearer your vision, the more powerful your motivation will be.

Psychologist Dr. Gail Matthews conducted a study at Dominican University that found people who write down their goals are 42% more likely to achieve them than those who don't. Writing forces clarity. It transforms abstract hopes into concrete objectives.

Once your vision is on paper, take it further—engage with it emotionally. Close your eyes and imagine your future self. What do you feel? What does your daily life look like? How do you carry yourself? Neuroscience has shown that when you mentally rehearse your goals, your brain begins to see them as inevitable, making you more likely to take the necessary actions to achieve them.

Clarity breeds action. The more detailed your five-year vision, the easier it becomes to bridge the gap between where you are now and where you want to be.

## Reverse-Engineering Success into Daily Actions

Big goals can be intimidating. The reason so many people abandon their ambitions is simple: they look at the entire mountain instead of focusing on the next step. The solution? Reverse-engineering.

Let's break it down. If your goal is to build a six-figure business in five years, what needs to happen in the next three years? The next one year? The next six months? The next week? By working backward from the outcome, you create a roadmap that makes success achievable.

You can apply this to your own aspirations.

- Identify the key milestones that lead to your five-year vision.
- Break those milestones into monthly objectives.
- Distill them further into weekly and daily actions.

For instance, if you aim to become financially independent, you might start by learning about investing (daily habit), increasing your income streams (monthly goal), and automating your savings and investments (system-level strategy).

By focusing on small, consistent actions, you eliminate overwhelm and build momentum. Progress compounds. A single intentional hour per day accumulates into 1,825 hours of mastery over five years. That's the difference between wishing for success and systematically building it.

## Building a System That Guarantees Progress

Motivation is unreliable. Systems are not.

Too often, people rely on fleeting bursts of inspiration to drive progress, only to burn out when motivation fades. The solution? Automate success by creating a structured system that keeps you on track—even on days when you don't feel like showing up.

A well-designed system consists of three core elements:

1. **Tracking Progress** – What gets measured gets managed. Create a habit tracker, journal, or digital dashboard to monitor your progress. Seeing tangible results fuels momentum.

2. **Accountability Structures** – **Public accountability increases success rates by up to 65%.** Find a mentor, join a mastermind group, or have an accountability partner who holds you to your commitments.

3. **Built-In Adjustments** – No plan is perfect from the start. Schedule regular check-ins (weekly or monthly) to assess your progress, identify obstacles, and refine your approach. Adaptability ensures long-term consistency.

Take, for example, athletes in Olympic training. They don't rely on motivation to train—they have structured routines, coaching feedback loops, and progress markers that guarantee improvement. Apply this same rigor to your own ambitions.

Building a system makes success inevitable because it removes the need for willpower. You don't need to think about what to do next—the system handles it for you.

## 8.4 Accountability & Continuous Growth

Personal transformation goes beyond singular breakthroughs—it's an ongoing commitment that endures even when life grows complicated or motivation dips. Those who sustain success aren't the ones who rely on short surges of willpower; they're the ones who establish systems that keep them evolving. There are three critical pillars to ensure you never cease growing: self-accountability, placing yourself among empowering influences, and embracing lifelong learning.

## How to Hold Yourself Accountable for Life

Accountability isn't about waiting for lightning-bolt inspiration; it's about creating a framework in which your stated goals naturally become reality. Many find accountability challenging because they view it as an optional add-on rather than a foundational component of their daily habits.

One especially effective method of self-accountability is public commitment. Research in social psychology shows that declaring your objectives to others dramatically raises the chances you'll follow through. For those reentering society after incarceration or recovering from a major crisis, publicly sharing your aspirations—be it securing consistent employment, saving money, or finishing an educational program—can provide a potent push. The discomfort of letting others see you miss a target can be a strong deterrent against drifting off-course.

However, accountability extends beyond external forces; it also involves cultivating internal integrity. Wrestle with this question: *Do I trust myself to honor my commitments when no one is watching?* If that trust feels fragile, begin with small, non-negotiable steps. For instance, pledge to journal for five minutes every evening, set aside a modest portion of each paycheck for savings, or spend ten minutes each morning in quiet reflection. Every completed promise underlines your identity as someone who follows through.

A useful tool to reinforce these habits is habit tracking. Simply crossing off tasks on a calendar or logging them in an app fosters a mental reward cycle, sometimes referred to as the "streak effect." Once you visualize a consecutive chain of completed objectives, you become less inclined to break it. This approach can be especially meaningful for those transitioning back into the workforce or a community setting—seeing tangible progress day by day can counteract lingering doubt or external judgment.

Ultimately, lifelong accountability is about cherishing your commitments as if they're sacred. High achievers rarely debate with themselves about whether they'll do the tasks they promised; they carry them out precisely because they declared they would. Dr. Angela Duckworth, author of Grit, emphasizes that when individuals connect their daily actions with a larger sense of purpose—like stabilizing finances for a family or proving reliable after a criminal justice setback—they're more likely to stay consistent even when stressors arise. In essence, accountability transforms fleeting ambition into a persistent guiding principle.

## Finding Mentors and Role Models to Elevate You

No one achieves greatness in isolation. The right mentors and role models can accelerate your growth exponentially, providing wisdom, guidance, and a higher standard to strive toward.

But how do you find a great mentor? The first step is shifting your mindset: stop looking for a savior, and start looking for specific guidance. Too often, people wait for a single mentor to take them under their wing when, in reality, mentorship happens in layers. Your role models may come from books, podcasts, industry leaders, or personal connections. Instead of searching for one perfect guide, build a "mentor network"—a mix of influences that help you develop in different areas of life.

If you do seek out a mentor in person, approach them with value, not just requests. Successful people are busy, and they don't have time to entertain vague requests like, *Can you mentor me?* Instead, find a way to offer something in return. Maybe you help them with research, assist in a project, or simply show an eagerness to apply their advice with results.

For example, Tim Ferriss, author of *The 4-Hour Workweek*, talks about how he once secured a mentor by offering to test the person's new business strategies for free and report back with real-world data. That kind of initiative stands out.

Beyond direct mentorship, immerse yourself in the mindset of high achievers. Listen to their interviews, study their books, and absorb their strategies. Over time, you'll begin to internalize their ways of thinking, making their success principles your own. In the world of probation, it may be discouraged to associate with other individuals with felony convictions, but in reality, there are plenty of people out there who have restored their life, built businesses, and serve as great examples of fortitude and success. Many of whom may be eager to open doors for people who are starting over or just beginning in their recovery process. It's not always easy to find employment or housing with an offender label, so people with criminal histories carve their own paths and become the bosses and landlords themselves, creating networks of support.

## The Importance of Lifelong Learning and Adaptation

The world is not static—and neither should you be. The most successful individuals understand that the moment they stop learning, they stop growing.

Warren Buffett, who spends 80% of his day reading and thinking. When asked about the key to success, he once pointed to a stack of books and said, "Read 500 pages like this every day. That's how knowledge works. It builds up, like compound interest."

Lifelong learning isn't just about reading—it's about actively seeking challenges that force growth. When you only engage in what you're already good at, you stagnate. The best way to remain adaptable is to deliberately put yourself in situations that force you to evolve. This could mean:

- **Learning a new skill outside your comfort zone**—whether it's coding, public speaking, or a foreign language.

- **Surrounding yourself with people who challenge your thinking**—instead of staying in an echo chamber.

- **Regularly updating your knowledge in your field**—because industries change, and staying relevant means staying ahead.

In today's fast-moving world, adaptability is the new competitive advantage. Those who are willing to reinvent themselves—again and again—are the ones who thrive.

# Chapter 8 Case Study: Dr. Stanley Andrisse

## Background:

Dr. Stanley Andrisse grew up in Ferguson, Missouri, an area later known for significant civil unrest. At a young age, he became involved in drug-related activities, leading to his first arrest at 14. By his early twenties, Andrisse had accumulated multiple felony convictions. In 2001, he was sentenced to 10 years in a maximum-security prison for drug trafficking offenses.

## Application of Principles:

- **Embracing a Growth Mindset:** While incarcerated, Andrisse sought personal development through education. He connected with mentors and immersed himself in scientific studies, particularly focusing on endocrinology and diabetes research, inspired by his father's battle with Type 2 diabetes.

- **Pursuing Education and Skill Development:** Upon release, Andrisse faced numerous rejections from doctoral programs due to his criminal record. However, with the support of a former college professor, he was admitted to Saint Louis University, where he earned a MBA and a PhD, completing his doctoral studies at the top of his class two years earlier than expected.

- **Advocacy and Mentorship:** Recognizing the challenges faced by formerly incarcerated individuals, Andrisse founded the nonprofit organization From Prison Cells to PhD. This initiative mentors and supports formerly incarcerated individuals in pursuing higher education and professional careers, aiming to dismantle barriers and promote successful reintegration.

## Notable Achievements:

- **Academic and Professional Roles:** Dr. Andrisse serves as an assistant professor of endocrinology at Howard University College of Medicine and has held positions at Georgetown Medical Center and Johns Hopkins Medicine. His research focuses on Type 2 diabetes and insulin resistance.

- **Authorship:** He authored the memoir *From Prison Cells to PhD: It Is Never Too Late to Do Good,* detailing his transformative journey from incarceration to academia.

- **Advocacy and Leadership:** Through his nonprofit, Andrisse has become a prominent advocate for educational opportunities for formerly incarcerated individuals, challenging policies that hinder their access to higher education and professional development.

## Outcome:

Dr. Stanley Andrisse's transformation from a convicted felon to a respected scientist and educator exemplifies the power of resilience, education, and mentorship. His commitment to supporting others with similar backgrounds highlights the potential for redemption and the importance of second chances.

# 8.5 Final Action Plan – Locking in Your New Life

Transformation is not a singular event—it's a commitment to continuous evolution. The work you've done to rewire your mindset, build discipline, and create a success-driven life will only last if you make it non-negotiable. Without structure, even the strongest willpower fades. Without a system, even the best intentions unravel. This final action plan is about making sure your new life doesn't slip away but instead solidifies into an unshakable foundation.

**Weekly Transformation Plan**

1.  **Week 1: Define Your Non-Negotiables (30 minutes):**

    *   Identify the behaviors and mindsets that you refuse to compromise on. These could include starting your mornings without social media, committing to never making excuses, or refusing to let fear dictate your decisions.

    *   Write down these non-negotiables and tie them to your identity rather than motivation. For example:

        *   Instead of saying, "I will try to work out every day," say, "I am the kind of person who prioritizes my health no matter what."

    *   Reflect on how these non-negotiables align with your new identity.

2.  **Week 2: Implement the 48-Hour Reset Rule (2 days):**

    *   Any time you feel yourself losing momentum, set aside two days to recenter yourself.

        *   **Day 1:** Spend in reflection—identify what threw you off course. Was it stress? Lack of structure? External distractions?

        *   **Day 2:** Spend in intentional action—recommit to your non-negotiables, even if it's just one small act.

    *   Celebrate each small victory along the way.

3.  **Week 3: Establish an Anchor Ritual (15 minutes):**

    *   Choose a small but powerful habit that instantly signals a fresh start. For some, it's cleaning their space; for others, it's journaling a new commitment.

    *   Practice this ritual whenever you feel stuck to signal a reset to your brain.

    *   Reflect on how this ritual helps you regain momentum.

4. **Week 4:** Reaffirm Your Commitment (30 minutes):

   - Ask yourself: Who am I choosing to become? Not just today, but for life.

   - Reaffirm this commitment regularly to strengthen the neural pathways that make success effortless.

   - Celebrate each time you act in alignment with your new identity.

5. **Daily Reflection and Accountability (5 minutes):**

   - Take a few minutes each day to reflect on your progress and align your actions with your non-negotiables.

   - Share your progress with an accountability partner to maintain motivation.

## Monthly Reflection and Adjustment

- **Assess Your Progress:** Take time to reflect on how far you've come. Identify areas where you've improved and where you still need to work.

- **Adjust Your Plan:** Based on your reflections, adjust your weekly habits to better align with your transformation goals.

## Additional Strategies for Success

1. **Forgive Yourself Quickly:** When you slip, don't let guilt paralyze you. Instead, reset and move forward.

2. **Celebrate Small Wins:** Acknowledge and celebrate each small victory along the way. This helps build confidence and reinforces positive behaviors.

3. **Surround Yourself with Support:** Engage with people who support and encourage your transformation. This could include joining a support group or finding a mentor.

By following this action plan, you'll begin to solidify your transformation into a lasting part of who you are, ensuring that your new life becomes an unshakable foundation for success.

## Chapter 8 Summary: Making Success Automatic – How to Sustain Your Transformation

Success isn't something you achieve once and then set aside—it's a way of life. True transformation isn't about willpower or temporary motivation—it's about creating a reality where growth becomes automatic. The systems, habits, and identity shifts you've built throughout this journey ensure that success is no longer a goal—it's your default mode of living.

You've learned that the greatest obstacle to lasting change isn't a lack of ambition—it's the failure to design an environment that supports your evolution. Without structure, even the strongest motivation fades. But when you build a lifestyle that reinforces resilience, discipline, and accountability, setbacks no longer derail you—they become stepping stones toward even greater growth.

By shifting from short-term effort to identity-based habits, you've rewired your brain to sustain transformation effortlessly. Your five-year vision isn't just a dream—it's a reality you've started engineering, step by step. Through habit stacking, structured execution, and a commitment to continuous learning, you've ensured that your progress doesn't stall but instead becomes a self-sustaining cycle of success.

At the core of lasting transformation is accountability and continuous growth. Surrounding yourself with the right people—mentors, role models, and like-minded individuals—will keep you moving forward even when challenges arise. Growth is not a destination; it's a commitment to refining, adapting, and expanding your potential every day.

The true test of success isn't whether you can change for a moment—it's whether you can build a life where growth never stops. You've done the work.

You've broken the cycles. You've rewritten your story. Now, the question is no longer *"Can I change?"* but *"What will I do with this transformation?"*

Because from here on out—success isn't something you chase. It's something you sustain.

# Conclusion

# The Path Forward—Becoming the Architect of Your Own Success

Throughout these chapters, we've navigated the complexities of transformation, shedding layers of self-doubt, dismantling outdated mental scripts, and cultivating a mindset built for enduring success. What began as a deep dive into reshaping your thoughts has blossomed into a strategic map for reclaiming your life—one intention, one disciplined action, and one courageous choice at a time.

## A Process, Not an Event

If there's a single theme echoing across these pages, it's this: true change isn't a one-time revelation—it's a continuous journey. Far too often, individuals hold onto the myth that a single moment of clarity or a sudden burst of motivation is all they need. Yet real progress unfolds through the daily commitment to rewire your mindset, align your behaviors, and reinforce the habits that make success inevitable—even under the weight of systemic barriers or past traumas.

## The Science and Strategy of Change

From the opening chapter, you learned that failure is rarely about lacking effort. Instead, invisible forces—subconscious fears, inherited beliefs, ingrained neural pathways—often shape behaviors more than we realize. Whether you spent years behind bars, faced persistent rejections in the workforce, or struggled with generational poverty, we uncovered how these patterns, though once deeply set, aren't immovable. Neuroplasticity—the brain's ability to adapt—proves that our mental "grooves" can indeed be redesigned.

We explored how fear and self-doubt aren't dead ends but signals pointing to the areas most ripe for growth. By reframing failure as feedback and letting go of perfectionism, you saw how forward motion is always available to anyone ready to take that next incremental step.

## The Systems That Sustain Success

Willpower alone was never designed to fuel a lifelong transformation. Systems matter—whether it's designing habits that eliminate distractions or strategically choosing an environment that fosters resilience. Self-discipline isn't about summoning Herculean strength each morning; it's an identity forged through consistent, smaller acts that build trust in yourself. Chapter 5's focus on productivity and focus redefined "doing more" as "doing what counts," refusing to let extraneous chaos drain your energy.

We then examined the environments that nourish or hinder growth, highlighting how toxic influences—be it negative peers, self-destructive habits, or constant reminders of past failures—can erode progress faster than any personal weakness. By selecting the people who surround you, setting firm boundaries, and actively shaping your atmosphere, you establish a protective ecosystem where growth feels sustainable rather than sporadic.

Yet no strategy, no matter how refined, endures unless it's woven into the fabric of your life. Hence the final chapter on locking in transformation, making success part of your identity. When you see yourself not as someone merely aiming to become disciplined or confident, but as someone who is disciplined and confident, the shift from effortful striving to inherent lifestyle truly begins.

## The Wealth and Confidence Mindset

Success doesn't rest on willpower and discipline alone; it also thrives on how you approach finances and self-assurance.

- **Financial Mindset:** Chapter 6 highlighted how wealth building transcends income level; it's about mindset, strategy, and erasing internalized beliefs that money is unattainable or morally suspect.

Those who successfully accumulate wealth work smarter, continually educate themselves on financial literacy, and set up income streams that multiply over time—even if they're starting with modest means late in life.

- **Confidence Reimagined:** Chapter 7 then reframed confidence from some elusive gift into a muscle you strengthen with each new challenge. Rather than seeking constant external approval, genuine confidence emerges from proving to yourself, again and again, that you can adapt, recover, and thrive. If you've been labeled by society— due to a criminal record, repeated failures, or personal setbacks—this chapter revealed that self-worth is an internal measure, not something another person or institution can define.

## Your Final Commitment

Now you've seen the evidence, read the methods, and felt the call to act. But knowledge alone changes nothing unless it's followed by purposeful steps.

- **Your thoughts mold your world—what convictions are you reinforcing about who you are and what you deserve?**

- **Your fears are illusions awaiting dismantlement—which leap will you take to break them?**

- **Your system is your blueprint for success—how will you design routines that turn goals into unshakable progress?**

This is the juncture where some close the book, feeling inspired yet unsure how to proceed, waiting for the right moment to begin. The difference between those who thrive and those who remain on the threshold is one word: action. They don't wait for fear to subside or for external permission. They move forward with conviction, even when self-doubt lingers.

Ask yourself: What does your next right step look like?

- **It could be initiating a 30-day challenge to fortify new habits.**

- **It could be stepping back from negativity that drains you.**

- **It could be waking at sunrise tomorrow to establish a morning ritual that aligns your mindset with the transformation you've envisioned.**

Whatever that step may be, start now.

Growth isn't a final destination you reach; it's a continual series of upgrades— mentally, emotionally, and practically. The moment you vow to make this journey a permanent aspect of how you live, nothing remains the same. You shed the old story, no matter how entrenched it was, and walk into a future shaped by your own hands.

This is your turning point. You've built the momentum; you've encountered the tools. All that remains is to choose—will you forge ahead, no matter the obstacles, or let this moment pass unclaimed?

Commit to the path. Then watch as your life transforms, one decision at a time. You and I both deserve to lead good, successful, enjoyable, abundant, and positive lives from here on out. Let's do it!

www.ingramcontent.com/pod-product-compliance
Lightning Source LLC
Chambersburg PA
CBHW071741120626
46550CB00002B/611